Armies of the Hundred Years' War 1337–1453

Gabriele Esposito is a military historian who works as a freelance author and researcher for some of the most important publishing houses in the military history sector. In particular, he is an expert specializing in uniformology: his interests and expertise range from the ancient civilizations to modern post-colonial conflicts. During recent years, he has conducted and published several researches on the military history of the Latin American countries, with special attention on the War of the Triple Alliance and the War of the Pacific. He is among the leading experts on the military history of the Italian Wars of Unification and the Spanish Carlist Wars. His books and essays are published on a regular basis by Osprey Publishing, Winged Hussar Publishing and Libreria Editrice Goriziana. He is also the author of numerous military history articles appearing in specialized magazines such as *Ancient Warfare Magazine*, *Medieval Warfare Magazine*, *The Armourer*, *History of War*, *Guerres et Histoire*, *Focus Storia* and *Focus Storia Wars*.

Armies of the Hundred Years' War 1337–1453

History, Organization, Weapons, Equipment and Tactics

Gabriele Esposito

Pen & Sword
MILITARY

First published in Great Britain in 2025 by
Pen & Sword Military
An imprint of
Pen & Sword Books Limited
Yorkshire – Philadelphia

Copyright © Pen & Sword Books Limited, 2025

ISBN 978 1 39903 782 2

The right of Gabriele Esposito to be identified as
Author of this Work has been asserted by him in accordance
with the Copyright, Designs and Patents Act 1988.

A CIP catalogue record for this book is
available from the British Library

All rights reserved. No part of this book may be reproduced or
transmitted in any form or by any means, electronic or mechanical
including photocopying, recording or by any information storage and
retrieval system, without permission from the Publisher in writing.

Typeset by Mac Style
Printed and bound in India by Replika Press Pvt Ltd.

Pen & Sword Books Limited incorporates the imprints of After the Battle,
Atlas, Archaeology, Aviation, Discovery, Family History, Fiction, History,
Maritime, Military, Military Classics, Politics, Select, Transport, True Crime,
Air World, Frontline Publishing, Leo Cooper, Remember When, Seaforth
Publishing, The Praetorian Press, Wharncliffe Local History, Wharncliffe
Transport, Wharncliffe True Crime and White Owl.

For a complete list of Pen & Sword titles please contact:

PEN & SWORD BOOKS LIMITED
47 Church Street, Barnsley, South Yorkshire, S70 2AS, England
E-mail: enquiries@pen-and-sword.co.uk
Website: www.pen-and-sword.co.uk
or
PEN AND SWORD BOOKS
1950 Lawrence Rd, Havertown, PA 19083, USA
E-mail: uspen-and-sword@casematepublishers.com
Website: www.penandswordbooks.com

Contents

Acknowledgements vi
Introduction vii

Chapter 1   The Origins of the Anglo-French Rivalry   1

Chapter 2   The First Phase of the War, 1337–1354   44

Chapter 3   The Second Phase of the War, 1355–1389   70

Chapter 4   The Third Phase of the War, 1390–1428   96

Chapter 5   The Fourth Phase of the War, 1429–1453   117

Chapter 6   The Armies of the Hundred Years' War   133

Bibliography 190
The Re-enactors who Contributed to this Book 191
Index 196

Acknowledgements

This book is dedicated to my magnificent parents, Maria Rosaria and Benedetto, for the immense love and fundamental support that they always give me. This book would not have been possible without their precious advice deriving from long experience. A very special thanks goes to Philip Sidnell, the commissioning editor of my books for Pen & Sword: his love for history and his passion for publishing are key factors behind the success of our publications. Many thanks also to the production manager of this title, Matt Jones, for his excellent work and great enthusiasm. A special mention is due to Tony Walton for the magnificent work of editing that he makes for all my books. A very special mention goes to the brilliant re-enactment groups that collaborated with their photographs to the creation of this book: without the incredible work of research of their members, the final result of this publication would have not been the same. As a result, I want to express my deep gratitude to the following living history associations: Alliance des Lions d'Anjou, Alsatiae Protectores, Genz d'armes 1415, Genz d'ordonnance, La Guerre des Couronnes and Les Lions du Kent from France; The Free Company of Aquitaine from the United Kingdom; and Toxophilus.net from Germany.

Introduction

The main aim of this work is to present a detailed overview of the campaigns and armies of the Hundred Years' War, the long military conflict that opposed the Kingdom of England against the Kingdom of France during the late Middle Ages. In the first chapter of the book, we will reconstruct the development of the bitter Anglo-French rivalry, starting from the year 1066, which saw the start of the Norman Conquest of England. Indeed, it was with the ascendancy of William the Conqueror to the English throne that a vassal of the King of France – i.e. Duke William of Normandy – became King of England. We will see how during the period 1066–1337, before the outbreak of the Hundred Years' War, England and France fought several conflicts against each other. These comparatively little-known wars determined the development of a longstanding rivalry that erupted into a large-scale conflict in 1337. In the second chapter, we will deal with the campaigns of the first phase of the Hundred Years' War, most notably with the Battle of Crécy in 1346. The third chapter describes the campaigns of the second phase of the Hundred Years' War, including the decisive Battle of Poitiers in 1356. In the fourth chapter, we will focus on the campaigns of the third phase of the Hundred Years' War, paying particular attention to the decisive Battle of Azincourt in 1415. The fifth chapter deals with the campaigns of the fourth phase of the conflict, which culminated with the fall of English France in 1453. The sixth and final chapter of the book will be devoted to a description of the English and French armies that fought between 1337 and 1453, paying particular attention to the organization and equipment of the various military contingents. The latter will include some iconic troop types, such as the formidable English and Welsh longbowmen and the famous French heavy cavalry. As we will see from the analysis contained in the following pages, the Hundred Years' War was a great international conflict that involved most of Western Europe, playing a key role in the development of both England and France as modern nations.

Chapter 1

The Origins of the Anglo-French Rivalry

Henry I, fourth son of William the Conqueror, reigned until 1135 as the last of the Norman monarchs of England. Henry had just one legitimate son, William Adelin, who was to be his heir both as King of England and Duke of Normandy. In 1106, Henry I had been able to reconquer the French domains inherited from his famous father and thus reunited (albeit temporarily) the English and French territories of the Normans under the rule of a single monarch. In 1120, however, an unpredictable event had massive consequences: the heir to the throne, William Adelin, died when the royal vessel known as the *White Ship*, which was transporting him, sank en route from Normandy to England. This dramatic event was the beginning of a very complex phase in the history of the English lands, with King Henry being too old to generate a new male heir. The king had a legitimate daughter, Matilda, but in Medieval Europe it was very uncommon to have a woman inheriting a throne. However, having no other choice, during the years that followed 1120, Henry I designated Matilda as his successor, despite the opposition of a good portion of the English nobility. After her first husband, Henry V, monarch of the Holy Roman Empire, died in 1125, Matilda was remarried in 1128 to one of the most powerful French nobles, Geoffrey V, Count of Anjou. Geoffrey controlled extensive territories in north-western France and was one of the King of France's most powerful vassals. The County of Anjou bordered with the Duchy of Normandy, and the Angevins had long been the most fierce enemies of the Normans. The border between Normandy and Anjou had been the scene of several battles between the two aristocratic families, as a result of which Geoffrey V was hated by many of England's Norman nobility. Geoffrey had very ambitious political plans: he wanted to unite England, Normandy and Anjou into a single Angevin Empire stretching from the southern borders of Scotland to the very heart of France. During the years 1135–54, following the death of Henry I, Matilda and Geoffrey struggled to secure control of England against a large number of English nobles. This turbulent period, characterized by a series of civil wars, became known as 'The Anarchy', which ended on 19 December 1154 when the son of Matilda and Geoffrey was crowned as Henry II, King of England, at Westminster Abbey. By his side was his wife, Eleanor of Aquitaine.

2 Armies of the Hundred Years' War 1337–1453

Man-at-arms equipped with *bascinet* helmet and corselet consisting of riveted metal plates. (*Photo and copyright by Alliance des Lions d'Anjou*)

Man-at-arms equipped with *bascinet* and corselet obtained from boiled leather. (*Photo and copyright by Alliance des Lions d'Anjou*)

Henry II experienced the most serious of his military problems on the Continent, where he had a very difficult relationship with the King of France, Louis VII. The French king feared that the Angevin Empire could be a serious obstacle to the creation of a centralized monarchy in France, and saw Henry II as a great rival. In his early life, Henry II had already clashed with Louis VII, who refused to recognize him as the legitimate Duke of Normandy. This situation only worsened when Henry married Eleanor of Aquitaine, who had previously been Louis VII's wife and controlled vast swathes of French territory. Henry II created a strong network of alliances with some of the most important French nobles in order to secure his dominion over Normandy and Anjou. In addition to marrying Eleanor of Aquitaine, he concluded military alliances with the Counts of Flanders and Blois. From a military point of view, Henry was much stronger than Louis, so the French monarch never attempted to fight a full-scale war against him. For many years, however, France lived in a state of constant tension, the borders of the Angevin Empire being frequently raided by nobles who were allied with Louis VII. In 1154, soon after being crowned in Westminster, the new English king travelled to France and concluded a peace treaty with Louis. He returned some territories to the French monarch but did not pay homage to him as a vassal of the French crown (something that Henry was formally obliged to do because he was also the Duke of Normandy). In 1158, after several years of growing tension between the two kings, Henry II's eldest son (who would die a few years later) married Louis VII's daughter, Margaret. However, this union failed to end the ongoing 'cold war' between Henry and Louis. The English monarch had a clear political plan in his mind: he wanted to expand his territorial possessions in France as much as possible without fighting long wars. One of his primary targets was the Duchy of Brittany, located to the west of Normandy.

Brittany was largely independent from the crown of France and had a peculiar culture. It had long been inhabited by Celtic communities that had a lot in common with those in Wales, and had only been annexed to France by Charlemagne after some very costly military campaigns. The Bretons had their own language and traditions, which were very different from those of mainland France. Like Wales, Brittany was divided into a series of small princedoms, whose warlike rulers were never fully submitted by the central authority of the Duke of Brittany. In 1148, upon the death of Conan III, Duke of Brittany, a civil war broke out in the region. Henry II claimed to be the overlord of Brittany, since the region had earlier owed loyalty to his predecessor, Henry I. Consequently, Henry supported one of the two sides in the internecine conflict in order to have a new Duke of Brittany who would look favourably upon him. However, the pretender supported by Henry II (the future Conan IV) then changed his political line and started a struggle to preserve the autonomy of his homeland. As a result, the King of England also amended his political approach and occupied the County of Nantes in eastern Brittany in 1158. Louis VII of France did not directly intervene in the civil conflict in Brittany, as the region was part of the Angevins' sphere of political influence. Henry II operated not only in northern France but also in the south, where he attempted to enlarge his wife's possessions in Aquitaine. The important city of Toulouse, which had always been part of the Duchy of Aquitaine, had recently started to be ruled as an independent county. Henry, refusing to accept this state of affairs, concluded an alliance with the main enemy of Toulouse, Raymond Berenguer of Barcelona. The Count of Toulouse, Raymond V, tried to preserve the independence of his territories by forming an alliance with Louis VII of France: he married the latter's sister, Constance, in the hope of stopping Henry II's expansionism. The English king, however, attacked Toulouse and ravaged the countryside around the city before seizing several nearby castles and annexing the region of Quercy to Aquitaine. Although Henry II and Louis VII still did not wage open war against each other, tensions between the two monarchs continued to grow.

After Henry II started to show his belligerency in Aquitaine, Louis VII decided to reinforce his political position by forming new alliances with important French aristocrats. After the death of his wife, Louis married the sister of the counts of Blois and Champagne. The latter were extremely powerful and controlled two of France's richest regions. The County of Blois was ruled by Theobald V and the County of Champagne by Henry I. Theobald had previously been an ally of Henry II, but was increasingly worried by the expansionist ambitions of the Angevins. When Theobald mobilized his military forces along the border with Henry II's French possessions, the English king responded by attacking the territory of Blois and seizing the count's main castle after a lengthy siege. As 1161 dawned, total war between Henry II and Louis VII seemed inevitable, but during the following year a peace treaty was arranged between the two kings thanks to the mediation of Pope Alexander III. This treaty simply ratified the situation existing on the ground and could thus be considered as a personal victory by Henry II. The English king had been able to expand and stabilize the Angevin Empire without fighting a large-scale war. Henry II's dominions did not have a coherent organization and were not under the control of a single government, instead consisting of a loose and highly flexible network of feudal connections that were all linked to the Angevin family. Henry travelled widely across his empire, confirming his direct or indirect control over its various components and reforming the local governments in order to make them more efficient. Henry could count on the support of an emerging class of 'new men', minor aristocrats who were capable administrators and who rose to positions of prominence thanks to their personal

Man-at-arms wearing a padded *aketon* over his metal cuirass and a *bascinet*. He is armed with a war hammer. (*Photo and copyright by Alliance des Lions d'Anjou*)

Man-at-arms armed with a deadly falchion sword.
(*Photo and copyright by Alliance des Lions d'Anjou*)

loyalty towards the monarch. It was thanks to them that the Angevin Empire was kept together by Henry II, despite the opposition of several powerful barons. From 1164, Louis VII of France started to enlarge his anti-Angevin coalition by forming alliances with the Duchy of Burgundy and the new Count of Flanders.

In 1165, Louis finally had a male heir, the future Philip Augustus, and thus secured his own position as King of France in view of any future claim over his throne coming from the Angevins. Meanwhile, Henry II had started to exert a more direct control over Brittany, launching a large-scale invasion of the region in 1166. The English king forced Conan IV to abdicate as duke and gave Brittany to Conan's daughter, Constance, who was betrothed to Henry II's son, Geoffrey. With this move, the English king showed his firm intention to include Brittany among the territories of the Angevin Empire. Henry II continued to act in other areas of France, most importantly in Aquitaine, where he prolonged his struggle with Raymond of Toulouse. He could now count on the support of the Archbishop of Bordeaux, as well as of Alfonso II of Aragon. As a result, Raymond of Toulouse was forced to divorce from Louis VII's sister and came under the political influence of Henry II. In 1167, following these events, open war finally broke out between the Angevin monarch and the King of France. Louis VII allied himself with the Kingdom of Scotland, the Welsh princedoms and the Bretons in the hope of crushing the empire of his rival. Normandy was attacked by French troops, but Henry II responded with a violent counter-attack that destroyed the main logistical base of his enemy at Chaumont-sur-Epte. After this defeat, before the war could become more widespread, Louis VII abandoned his allies and made a truce with the English king. Henry was thereafter free to crush the Bretons and restore his rule over the crucially important duchy. During the following years, the English monarch became increasingly concerned about the succession to his throne, deciding that his empire would be divided into three parts after his death: his first son, Henry, was to receive England and Normandy, while Richard (the future 'Lionheart') was given the Duchy of Aquitaine and Geoffrey the Duchy of Brittany. In 1169, the king met with his old rival Louis VII at Montmirail, where the French monarch recognized Henry's plans for the division of his domains as legitimate, in exchange for receiving formal homage from Henry's sons. The years following the peace agreement signed at Montmirail saw the King of England reinforcing his position in southern France, concluding an alliance with the Count of Savoy in the east and the King of Castile in the west. The daughter of the Count of Savoy was promised to Henry II's other son, John (later known as 'John Lackland'), while the Castilian monarch married Henry's daughter, Eleanor.

In 1180, the King of France and longstanding enemy of Henry II, Louis VII, died and was replaced on the throne in Paris by his ambitious son, Philip Augustus. Philip

The Origins of the Anglo-French Rivalry 9

Man-at-arms equipped with a stecktarge, or jousting shield. An embroidered torse or orle (a band of coloured cloth wrapped around the helmet), like the one shown here, was often applied on the external surface of the helmet. (*Photo and copyright by Alliance des Lions d'Anjou*)

Man-at-arms wearing an early form of hounskull *bascinet*.
(*Photo and copyright by Alliance des Lions d'Anjou*)

was determined to destroy the Angevin Empire and was ready to use the frictions existing within the English royal family to his advantage. In 1186, the new French monarch asked Henry II for permission to have custody of Geoffrey's children (Henry's son having died that year) and of the Duchy of Brittany. Philip clearly wanted to expel the Angevins from the French fiefdom. If the King of England rejected Philip's request, French forces threatened to attack Normandy. Since no agreement was found, both sides mobilized their troops and an indecisive clash took place before the intervention of the Pope, who sponsored a truce. During the ensuing negotiations, King Philip tried to convince Richard to join his cause, but with little success. Henry II was at the time still too strong to be defeated. Meanwhile, during 1187, the holy city of Jerusalem was conquered by Saladin and calls for a new crusade swept Europe. Richard was enthusiastic about the idea of organizing a crusade, but neither Henry II nor Philip Augustus had any intention of wasting their time in what they considered a futile military enterprise. Richard, as 'junior monarch' of England, started to raise taxes and make plans for an expedition to the Holy Land, but his preparations were opposed by his father. Meanwhile, he also stabilized his position in Aquitaine by attacking the Count of Toulouse, who was a loyal ally of Philip Augustus. Richard's military initiative, which had not been authorized by his father, led to the outbreak of a new conflict between the Angevin Empire and France. Henry II, wanting to avoid a new large-scale conflict with Philip, tried to convince the latter to agree to a long-term peace deal. The young French monarch rejected the offer and hostilities commenced, albeit at a low intensity.

In 1188, Richard finally abandoned his father and joined Philip Augustus, giving formal homage to the French king as Duke of Normandy. Wishing to free the Holy Land from the Muslims, the papacy then intervened again and a new peace conference was organized in 1189. By that time, Henry II was suffering from a severe bleeding ulcer and his health was deteriorating very rapidly. The peace talks achieved very little, Henry revealing his intention to cede his main possessions to his younger son, John, and not to Richard as agreed previously. After the diplomatic meetings ended, Philip and Richard launched a surprise attack against Henry II's forces in France. The King of England had no choice but to retreat to Normandy, where he prepared to face an enemy offensive. During most of his life, the Angevin monarch had been a great military leader, and in this campaign – which was going to be his last one – he showed all his old capabilities. Instead of defending the borders of Normandy, as expected by his opponents, he turned south towards Anjou to launch a counter-offensive. Here, however, his health worsened rapidly. Before the king died, he was visited by Richard. Father and son had a last meeting, where some sort of reconciliation took place and Richard was again designated as the future King of England. Shortly after having been informed that his favourite son, John, had also sided with Richard and Philip, King Henry II died at Chinon on 6 July 1189. Shortly after these events, both Richard of England and Philip of France participated in the Third Crusade, during which they fell into dispute on several occasions. In 1192, on his way back to England, Richard the Lionheart was captured by the Duke of Austria, Leopold V, who had participated in the Third Crusade and had established a solid alliance with Philip Augustus. After being ransomed in 1193, Richard had to return hastily to England, where his younger brother, John, had practically usurped the throne. After having restored order in his kingdom, Richard went to France in order to fight against Philip Augustus. The French king had attacked Normandy during Richard's captivity and had occupied the region of Vexin. Richard spent the following years building new castles in Normandy and skirmishing with French troops. At the same time, he organized a large alliance against Philip Augustus that comprised Baldwin IX, Count of Flanders, and King Sancho VI of Navarre. On the field, Angevin forces obtained several victories over the French. Philip's forces were defeated at the Battle of Fréteval in 1194 and later at the larger Battle of Gisors in 1198. The latter saw a clash between 200 English knights and 300 French nobles, which was decided by an audacious charge led by the Lionheart. In March 1199, Richard moved to Limousin in order to suppress a revolt by the local ruler, Aimar V of Limoges. King Richard was struggling to keep the Angevin Empire united, recognizing that Philip Augustus's main target was the Duchy of Normandy. As a result, he employed all his resources and personal energies to secure his position in northern France. On 26 March, however, while besieging a castle in Limousin, Richard was hit in the shoulder by the dart of a crossbow. The wound, which initially seemed curable, rapidly turned gangrenous and the king's condition worsened. On 6 April 1199, in the arms of his mother, Eleanor of Aquitaine, Richard the Lionheart died.

Since the king had no legitimate heirs, he was succeeded as King of England by his brother, John. The French territories of the Angevins rejected John's rule, an act that marked the beginning of the end for the empire created by Henry II. Upon Richard's death, there were two potential claimants to the English throne: John and the young Arthur I of Brittany, who was the son of John's elder brother, Geoffrey. John, however, was supported by most of the English aristocrats and by his mother, Eleanor of Aquitaine, and was duly crowned in Westminster Abbey soon after the death of his brother. Arthur was supported by the nobles of Brittany, Maine and Anjou, and also had an ally in Philip Augustus, who was determined to continue his campaigns in Normandy against the new English monarch. Soon after becoming king, John had to defend the Duchy of Normandy from the assaults of Arthur and Philip. He could count on the excellent castles that had been built by his brother as well as on the network of regional alliances that had been created by the Lionheart. Since neither side was able to gain the upper hand in the hostilities, John and Philip met to negotiate terms for peace in January 1200 (being under strong pressure from the papacy). The subsequent Treaty of Le Goulet was signed some months later,

Man-at-arms equipped with a hounskull *bascinet*.
(*Photo and copyright by Alsatiae Protectores*)

Man-at-arms wearing an open *bascinet* and armed with an axe.
(*Photo and copyright by Genz d'armes 1415*)

according to which Philip recognized John as the legitimate heir of Richard's French possessions and John recognized Philip as his feudal overlord in France. The new peace, however, was very short-lived, with both sides resuming hostilities in 1202. At the beginning of the new war, King John adopted a defensive attitude, avoiding pitched battles against the French and limiting himself to defending his strong castles. Normandy was now attacked by two armies: a French one under Philip Augustus and a Breton one led by Arthur. After various indecisive engagements, John decided to face Arthur on the open field and defeated him at the Battle of Mirebeau on 31 July 1202. This was John's first important victory, the king managing to capture Arthur and most of his supporters. The young Duke of Brittany was killed several months later in order to eliminate a dangerous potential rival for John.

At this point of the war, John started to experience serious difficulties. As his armies were mostly made up of mercenaries recruited from Flanders and Brabant, his financial resources were becoming seriously stretched, and he was not able to secure control over the territories that had supported Arthur. Over time, an increasing number of Angevin nobles, who had previously been loyal to Richard the Lionheart, started to abandon John. With Arthur's death and with King John experiencing serious military difficulties, they saw Philip Augustus as their possible new overlord. By that time, the King of France was besieging Chateau Gaillard, the strongest fortification built by King Richard to defend the borders of Normandy. John attempted to relieve the besieged garrison in the latter part of 1203, but his counter-offensive failed. The frustrated English monarch then moved to Brittany, where the local population had started revolting against him. John crushed the Breton revolt with great determination, but could do little to improve his general military situation: Philip Augustus, who could count on large feudal military forces, was gradually gaining the upper hand. In March 1204, after a long and complex siege, Chateau Gaillard was taken by the French. Several weeks later, John suffered another blow when Eleanor of Aquitaine died. John's forces in Normandy tried to establish a new defensive line after the fall of their main stronghold, but Philip Augustus was able to move around their defences and launch a devastating offensive against the very heart of Normandy. By August 1204, the King of France had conquered the whole of Normandy and could continue his advance. He then invested Anjou and Poitou, which were occupied quite easily by the French thanks to the collaboration of the local nobles. By the end of the year, of the Angevin Empire's French territories, only the Duchy of Aquitaine remained in John's hands.

The military disasters of 1203–04 significantly weakened the international position of the King of England, who had to secure the sea route connecting Aquitaine to England following the loss of the land one that crossed Normandy. In addition, John had to secure England against a potential French invasion. He reorganized his feudal forces in order to have a number of permanent troops at his disposal and built many new warships in an attempt to control the Channel. By 1212, King John could count on a large fleet of over 100 ships, made up of three main components:

Man-at-arms equipped with an open *bascinet*. (*Photo and copyright by Alsatiae Protectores*)

royal galleys built during the previous years, smaller warships provided by the Cinque Ports and merchant ships converted to military use. John's new fleet was commanded by William of Wrotham and had Portsmouth as its main operational base. The new naval resources assembled by John, however, were mostly used for defensive purposes. Indeed, instead of attempting a landing in Normandy, William of Wrotham was tasked with protecting the southern coast of England from any attack organized by the French. King John wanted to reconquer Normandy by attacking it from the south. His plan was to raise substantial land forces in Aquitaine and to use these to attack the French in Poitou (a key region located north of Aquitaine and south of Normandy). In 1206, John went to Poitou to organize his offensive, but he was forced

The Origins of the Anglo-French Rivalry 17

Louis III, Duke of Anjou (1403–1434). (*Photo and copyright by Alliance des Lions d'Anjou*)

to fight a minor campaign on the southern border of Aquitaine against Alfonso VIII of Castile. After wasting some precious time, the English king finally attacked in Poitou and took the important city of Angers. When Philip Augustus moved south to intercept John, the campaign ended in stalemate and a truce of two years was stipulated between the two kings. This brief period of peace was employed by John to gather more financial resources for a further attack on Normandy. The English monarch also concluded several important military alliances, with Otto IV (a pretender to the crown of Holy Roman Emperor) and with a handful of major French aristocrats (Renaud of Boulogne and Ferdinand of Flanders, among others).

In 1213, Philip Augustus took the initiative before John and sent his elder son, Louis, to invade Flanders. His plan was to take control of the important Flemish ports in order to organize an invasion of England. John was forced to use his new fleet for the first time and launched a pre-emptive strike against the French naval forces that were anchored in the harbour of Damme. The English raid was successful, resulting in the destruction of most of Philip's vessels and the abandonment of French plans to invade England. In 1214, King John organized his last military campaign in continental Europe, with the objective of taking Normandy back from Philip Augustus. This time he appeared to have a good chance of success, since he had been able to organize a very strong anti-French military alliance. Otto IV had finally been proclaimed Holy Roman Emperor by many of the German princes, and was now ready to help his English ally with substantial military resources. Renaud of Boulogne and Ferdinand of Flanders, being extremely worried about their king's plans for political centralization, were also determined to fight on King John's side. The English monarch developed a very complex military plan. John, at the head of an army mostly made up of mercenaries, would attack from Aquitaine by crossing Poitou and would menace the city of Paris. Meanwhile, his three allies (Otto, Renaud and Ferdinand) would assemble an army and attack the French from the north-east. The allied forces operating in Flemish territory were supported by an English contingent commanded by William Longespée, Earl of Salisbury, one of John's most loyal and experienced military commanders. Initially, everything worked well for King John. Moving from Aquitaine, he outmanoeuvred the French forces facing him, which were commanded by Prince Louis of France. As a result, the English were able to reconquer the County of Anjou by the end of June. Meanwhile, in the north, Philip Augustus had to mobilize his military forces very rapidly in order to face the menace posed by Otto's large army.

The opposing forces met on 27 July on the plain of Bouvines, where one of the largest and most important battles of the Middle Ages was fought. Philip Augustus's army consisted of around 1,300 heavily armed knights (of whom 765 came from the lands of the royal domain) and 300 'mounted sergeants', supported by 3,160 infantrymen provided by the municipalities of northern France. The King of France could also count on 2,000 mercenary infantry, and his forces numbered a total of some 6,700 men. These were deployed on the field of battle into three divisions, known as 'battles' in medieval military terminology. The right battle consisted of knights from Champagne, Burgundy and Picardy, as well as 150 mounted sergeants from Soissons. The central battle comprised the knights from the lands of the royal domain as well as the foot militiamen sent by the northern French towns. The left battle consisted of Breton knights and other foot militiamen provided by the municipalities. Behind the French army was the bridge of Bouvines, the only means of retreat across the local marshes of the area, guarded by another 150 mounted sergeants. The Imperial army of Otto comprised around 1,500 knights (including 650 from Flanders and 500 from Hainaut) and 7,500 footmen (including several hundred English archers). Like Philip Augustus, the Holy Roman Emperor divided his troops into three divisions or battles. The left battle consisted of Flemish knights, supported by foot soldiers from Flanders and Hainaut. The central battle consisted of Saxon knights as well as infantrymen from Germany and Brabant (who were equipped with long pikes). The right battle comprised English knights and foot soldiers from Brabant, and was commanded by William Longespée. The English archers were deployed as a reserve on the extreme right flank of the Imperial army.

The Battle of Bouvines began with an attack by the French right flank, launched by the 150 lightly armoured mounted sergeants against the Flemish knights opposing them. This assault was easily repulsed by Otto's men, but was followed by a second attack led by the knights of Champagne. This was also stopped by the Flemish knights, who then took the initiative. To stop the Flemish advance, the French had to launch several frontal charges with all their knights of the left division, and the enemy ranks were finally broken after three hours of bitter fighting. In the centre, the French urban militiamen were easily crushed by Otto's elite German knights. The French monarch, who was in the centre of his line, was unhorsed during this phase of the battle, and was saved only with great difficulty by his knights. In this sector too, the French had to launch several frontal charges with all their available knights until Otto's men were pushed back. The emperor ran the risk of being captured, and his personal banner was taken by the French knights. On the Imperial left, William Longespée, after some initial success, was unhorsed and captured: his soldiers, demoralized, fled from the battlefield after having seen very little action. When the allied forces started to abandon the battlefield, a force of 700 pikemen from Brabant resisted alone against the advancing French, forming a defensive ring. The Imperial infantrymen, led by Reginald of Boulogne, repulsed all the attacks of the

Man-at-arms with a hounskull *bascinet*. (*Photo and copyright by La Guerre des Couronnes*)

Man-at-arms wearing a *camail* made of metal scales. (*Photo and copyright by La Guerre des Couronnes*)

Man-at-arms with a *camail* of metal scales. (*Photo and copyright by La Guerre des Couronnes*)

French cavalry and gained some precious time for the retreat of their comrades until being completely crushed. The Battle of Bouvines was a decisive victory for Philip Augustus: the enemy army that invaded northern France was completely destroyed, and King John's plans were frustrated. Having no hope of successfully continuing his campaign from Aquitaine, the English king made peace with his French rival. Anjou was returned to Philip, and John even paid compensation to the King of France. The Battle of Bouvines also had important consequences for the political situation of England, as it destroyed all hopes for a restoration of the Angevin Empire. King John's position became extremely precarious in his home realm, the English barons being ready to take advantage of the situation in order to pursue their own interests.

In 1215, several leading English nobles revolted against King John in what became known as the First Barons' War. At one point of the conflict, fearing that defeat was quite near for them, the English nobles invited Louis of France to join them. The son of Philip Augustus planned to land in southern England in May 1216, so John sent his powerful fleet to intercept him. Unfortunately for the king, however, a series of storms dispersed his warships and the French were able to land unopposed in Kent. The region was easily conquered by Louis, including the important royal castles of Canterbury and Rochester. On 25 July, the Anglo-French forces of the barons moved to the key castle of Dover, which was well-supplied and had a large garrison. The siege of the stronghold lasted for three months, but Louis was forced to abandon it in order to move on London. The castles at Windsor and Lincoln also resisted the besieging operations of the Anglo-French forces. When a pitched battle between John and Louis seemed imminent, King Alexander II of Scotland invaded northern England and the royal army had to move north in order to intercept the Scottish forces (which had already occupied Carlisle). Being unable to crush the invading Scots and occupy London before the arrival of Louis, John fell back to Winchester, where he started reorganizing his forces. The French prince entered London after encountering very little resistance and was soon proclaimed (though not crowned) King of England. Alexander II of Scotland was present at the ceremony and gave homage to Louis, since he had important fiefdoms in England. As time progressed, however, many barons started to change their attitude towards their foreign ally. They had initially invited the French because they wanted to defeat John, but now England was running the risk of becoming a domain of Philip Augustus. Several of the most powerful nobles who had previously abandoned King John, including William Longespée, switched sides and rejoined the royalists. Despite the defection of some aristocrats who had initially supported him, Louis continued his conquest of England, advancing westwards to besiege the castle of Winchester. This was captured after ten days of fighting, but King John had already abandoned it.

Man-at-arms equipped with a *bascinet*. (*Photo and copyright by Alsatiae Protectores*)

Man-at-arms with a *bascinet*. (*Photo and copyright by La Guerre des Couronnes*)

Man-at-arms wearing a hounskull *bascinet*. (*Photo and copyright by La Guerre des Couronnes*)

In September 1216, John launched a strong counter-offensive, attacking eastwards between London and Cambridge in order to break up the positions of his enemies. While leading the offensive, however, the monarch contracted dysentery and fell ill. On 19 October 1216, the king died at the castle of Newark in Nottinghamshire. With his death, the main reason behind the outbreak of the ongoing conflict ceased to exist. The barons, having reached their objective without fighting a single pitched battle, now decided to expel the French and Louis from their territories. Prince Henry, the son and heir of King John, was a child aged just 9 and thus was not perceived as a threat like the foreign prince. Most of the barons abandoned their former French allies and crowned the youngster as Henry III in Gloucester Abbey. Louis still controlled London and a good portion of England, but his forces were now at a clear numerical disadvantage. During the last few weeks of 1216, Louis occupied several important castles, but in early 1217 he decided to return to his father's kingdom in search of reinforcements. To reach France, he had to cross Sussex and Kent, where a strong resistance movement had gradually developed: he was attacked on several occasions during his journey and was ambushed at Lewes. Louis lost many of his men during these minor clashes, but before he could leave England a new French fleet arrived with reinforcements and supplies. Now that the barons were his new enemies, Louis was becoming increasingly dependent on what could be sent to him from France by his father. Consequently, it was vital that he seized the port of Dover in order to use it as his main naval base. The French prince besieged the fortifications of Dover for a second time, but he was again unable to take them. While the French were concentrating their efforts against Dover, William Marshal attacked the forces of those barons who were still fighting for Louis near the castle of Lincoln in May 1217. In what became known as the Second Battle of Lincoln, 1,000 men assembled by William Marshal were able to defeat 1,600 pro-Louis soldiers who were besieging the castle (the garrison of which was loyal to Henry III). After the Second Battle of Lincoln, Louis decided to raise his second siege of Dover and went back to London with the reinforcements that he had received. Negotiations then took place between the French prince and William Marshal, but they came to nothing and hostilities resumed.

Some weeks later, there was a real turn in the tide when a new French fleet that had been sent to support Louis was defeated by English warships at the Battle of Sandwich on 24 August 1217. The French fleet was commanded by Eustace the Monk, an adventurer who once belonged to a monastic order before becoming a pirate. During the years 1205–08, Eustace and his companions worked for King John, who gave the pirate leader the Channel Islands and permitted him to use Winchelsea as his main base in England. In 1212, however, the former monk changed sides and started to serve Philip Augustus. It was thanks to Eustace that Louis landed in southern England to support the revolting barons and that the French captured the Cinque Ports. In the late summer of 1217, Philip Augustus sent a new fleet full of reinforcements and supplies to England, led by Eustace the Monk. The crews of the English warships built by King John now had a great opportunity to show their valour. They were commanded by Hubert the Burgh and had one precise order: to crush the French fleet that was sailing from Calais. Initially, the sailors from the Cinque Ports, who had been treated very badly by King John, had no intention to fight against the French, but they were eventually convinced to do so by the promise of being given great spoils should they destroy the French. Eustace the Monk, who was not formally the overall French commander, had eleven warships and seventy smaller transport vessels (which carried supplies). The English fleet had sixteen warships and twenty smaller auxiliary vessels. When the French armada sailed past Sandwich, the English fleet that was in the port came out and attacked it. Eustace was trying to reach the estuary of the Thames, his main objective being to reinforce Louis in London. Soon after the start of the clash, the English warships gained the windward position, which gave them a great advantage. The English warships were smaller than their French equivalents, but each of them had a contingent of archers, who killed many enemy sailors and soldiers from a distance before the

French bowmen embarked on Eustace's vessels could respond effectively. After some very hard fighting, the French flagship was boarded by the English and Eustace was captured; he was later executed as a traitor. Defeated, the remaining French warships returned to Calais. Most of the transport vessels, which were full of supplies, were captured by the English. The Battle of Sandwich, one of the greatest naval clashes of the Middle Ages, was decisive in determining the outcome of the First Barons' War. After such a defeat, with the English in full control of the Channel, Philip Augustus decided to stop supporting his son. Louis was totally cut off from France, abandoned by all his remaining English supporters. On 12 September 1217, a peace treaty was signed between the two warring parties at Kingston-upon-Thames. Louis formally renounced all his claims to the throne of England in return for being allowed to return to his country. Henry III, the new King of England, pardoned all the barons who had remained loyal to the French. England was again united and avoided foreign occupation. Henry III, however, experienced a series of internal problems during the following years, and his position became increasingly unstable. Hoping to take advantage of this situation, Louis of France, who had now been crowned king after the death of his father, decided to attack the English territorial possessions in Aquitaine (which were by now reduced to the regions of Poitou and Gascony). Poitou was easily conquered by the French, the local nobles having abandoned the young Henry III. Part of Gascony was also occupied, but in 1225 an English army was sent to France with orders to reconquer it. In exchange for providing their support to the reconquest of Gascony, the English barons obtained from Henry III the promulgation of an enlarged and improved version of the *Magna Carta* signed by King John.

In 1226, Louis of France died, leaving the throne to his young son, who became Louis IX. The rule of the 12-year-old King Louis was not accepted by some French nobles, which caused the outbreak of several revolts across the country. In 1228, some of the French aristocrats who were rebelling against Louis IX called upon Henry III to invade France. In particular, Peter I, Duke of Brittany, openly revolted against the young Louis and gave his homage to the King of England. Following these events, Henry III decided to invade France in 1230. He set sail from Portsmouth at the head of a large force of English troops, which landed at Saint-Malo in Brittany, where they joined forces with their French allies. Henry attacked the County of Anjou, but made little progress, then returned to Brittany before deciding to suspend his invasion of France, having understood the lack of strength in the support of the French nobles for his cause. During 1242 and 1243, Henry III was involved in a new French conflict known as the Saintonge War, from the name of the region where it was fought. Having been lost by King John, the County of Poitou had become part of the French territorial domains, and Louis of France had given it to his second

The Origins of the Anglo-French Rivalry   29

Man-at-arms wearing the padded protection that was placed under the *camail* of mail armour. (*Photo and copyright by La Guerre des Couronnes*)

Man-at-arms equipped for foot combat with halberd and rectangular shield.
(*Photo and copyright by La Guerre des Couronnes*)

son, Alphonse. The Poitevin barons opposed the idea of having the King of France's brother as their feudal overlord, and when Alphonse came of age, they revolted against him. The rebellion was led by the most powerful of the Poitevin nobles, Hugh X of Lusignan. The barons of Poitou wanted to have Richard of Cornwall, the younger brother of Henry III, as their count, and asked the English monarch to support them in their rebellion. Louis IX assembled a large army to help his brother and marched against the castle of Montreuil-Bonnin, which was the main stronghold of the Lusignan family. Meanwhile, Henry III assembled a force of 30,000 soldiers

Man-at-arms removing his helmet. (*Photo and copyright by Alsatiae Protectores*)

and set sail from Portsmouth. The King of England wanted to reconquer Poitou, considering it a first step towards the restoration of the empire that had been lost by his father. On 20 July 1242, a decisive battle between the forces of Henry III and Louis IX took place at Taillebourg, near the Charente river. Both sides deployed some 20,000 infantrymen, but the French had 4,000 heavy knights and the English just 1,600. The English attacked first, but they were soon repulsed. A subsequent counter-attack by the French knights was devastating and decided the outcome of the clash, with the strategic bridge crossing the Charente river being occupied by Louis IX's men. After their victory, the French took the rebel city of Saintes and obliged Hugh of Lusignan to surrender. Fearing that Louis IX could now also invest his possessions in Aquitaine, Henry III organized a naval blockade of the French port city of La Rochelle in order to distract some of the French troops. However, this operation also failed and the king was forced to ask for a truce. Following his defeat in the Saintonge War, Henry III had to abandon his plans to reconquer the Angevin lands in France. On 4 December 1259, he signed a lasting peace treaty with Louis IX in Paris, according to which the English monarch was given the territory of Guyenne in exchange for renouncing all his claims on other French lands.

The next English monarch to campaign in France was Edward I, who, despite internal opposition from clergymen and nobles, was able to fund a continental expedition in 1297. Three years before that, the Count of Flanders, Guy, had tried to conclude an alliance with Edward I by arranging a marriage between his daughter, Philippa, and the Prince of Wales. This, however, had been perceived as a menace to the stability of his realm by the new King of France, Charles IV, who imprisoned Guy and forced him to call off the planned marriage. The County of Flanders had a very special political status at the time: its rulers gave homage to both the King of France and the Holy Roman Emperor, and English merchants had some very strong commercial interests in Flemish lands. In 1296, the most important cities of Flanders were taken under French protection, at which point Guy asked for Edward I's help. However, in 1297 a large French army invaded the County of Flanders under orders to annex it to Charles IV's domains. Initially, the English tried to support their Flemish allies by attacking the French from Aquitaine, but their initiatives failed. As a result, in August 1297, Edward I landed with 900 knights and 7,500 infantrymen on the Flemish coast. After several weeks of fighting that saw no major engagements, the mediation of the Pope led to the signing of an armistice in October. Edward left the Continent without having achieved any significant result, mostly due to the fact that a major uprising had just begun in Scotland and the King of England had to deal with it.

The Origins of the Anglo-French Rivalry

Man-at-arms equipped with sword and triangular shield. (*Photo and copyright by La Guerre des Couronnes*)

In 1324, the new King of England, Edward II, was involved in a continental conflict against France that was known as the War of Saint-Sardos, from one of the locations around which it took place. Since 1322, there had been a new monarch in France, Charles IV, who acted much more aggressively towards English Gascony than his predecessor. In 1323, the French king demanded permission for his officials to carry out his royal orders on Gascon territory, a first step towards the annexation of Gascony to France and thus totally unacceptable to the English. After minor border skirmishes took place, Charles IV was ready to invade Gascony by the beginning of 1324. Edward II had just 4,500 knights and soldiers on the Continent, while the French assembled an army of 7,000 men. In retaliation for the French attack, the English king ordered the arrest of all French subjects who lived in England and seized all the English lands of his wife Isabella (who was Charles IV's sister). An English army of 11,000 soldiers was rapidly assembled and sent to the threatened territories, but Edward II had no intention of embarking on a long war against France. Indeed, he started negotiating with Charles IV in order to find a solution to the conflict. As part of the negotiations, the King of England was required to send her wife, Isabella, to Paris in 1325 as a diplomatic envoy. The English queen was able to find a compromise with which to end the

Man-at-arms armed with a sword. Note the complex decorations reproduced on the *vambraces* and greaves. (*Photo and copyright by La Guerre des Couronnes*)

Man-at-arms wearing a *bascinet*. (*Photo and copyright by Alsatiae Protectores*)

Man-at-arms with a highly-decorated cap made of felt. (*Photo and copyright by La Guerre des Couronnes*)

Man-at-arms equipped for foot combat, armed with a spiked polearm. (*Photo and copyright by Genz d'armes 1415*)

Man-at-arms armed with a sword. (*Photo and copyright by La Guerre des Couronnes*)

hostilities, but this was extremely favourable for her brother, Charles IV: Edward II would be required to give homage in person to the King of France in order to retain possession of Gascony. King Edward accepted the proposed terms but gave Gascony to his young son and heir, the future Edward III, so that it would be the Prince of Wales offering homage to Charles IV in Paris. Although the King of England was thus able to avoid a great international humiliation, he was about to be hit by an unexpected turn of events within his own family. His wife decided to remain in France, where she was involved in a relationship with one of her husband's exiled opponents, Roger Mortimer. Soon, all those who opposed Edward II began to gather around Isabella and Roger in Paris. The rebel couple, with the covert assistance of Charles IV, concluded a military alliance with William I, Count of Hainaut. Count William agreed to marry his daughter, Philippa, to the future Edward III (who had remained in France with his mother) and provided Roger Mortimer with a large fleet with which he could invade England. Soon after the marriage between Prince Edward and Philippa of Hainaut, Isabella and Roger started organizing their invasion of England. During August and September 1326, Edward II mobilized all the forces that were available to him and deployed his warships in the major English ports in order to prevent an enemy landing. He also sent a raiding force of 1,600 men across the Channel to perform a diversionary attack against Normandy.

On 24 September, Prince Edward, Isabella of France and Roger Mortimer landed in Suffolk at the head of a small military force, without meeting any resistance. They were soon joined by an increasing number of barons, who rose up in revolt against Edward II. The king, meanwhile, had to face an uprising of London's population and was forced to abandon his capital. He hoped to reach Wales, where he was sure that his local supporters would be able to raise a new royal army, but it soon became apparent that the monarch had no chance of success. The Church and the royal administration abandoned him and changed sides, while the number of barons supporting Prince Edward grew rapidly. The king tried to flee to Ireland with his last followers, but was captured in Wales and escorted back to England. All the barons agreed on one point: Edward II had to be deposed, but at that time there was no established legal procedure for removing a King of England from his throne. Adam Orleton, the Bishop of Hereford, made a series of public allegations about Edward II's conduct as a monarch, and in January 1327 Parliament convened at Westminster to decide the future of the king. Most of the English population, especially the crowds of London, supported Prince Edward's ascendancy to the throne, and the barons agreed that Edward II should be replaced by his son. The king was officially accused of incompetence and delegates were sent to convince the monarch to abdicate. A tearful Edward II finally agreed in order to permit the coronation of his son. On

Man-at-arms armed with a poleaxe. (*Photo and copyright by Genz d'armes 1415*)

Man-at-arms wearing a frog-mouthed great helm. (*Photo and copyright by Genz d'armes 1415*)

21 January 1327, Edward II ceased to be King of England, and Edward III was crowned in Westminster Abbey on 2 February. While these events took place in Britain, the political situation also started to change in continental Europe. There was a new monarch on the French throne, Philip VI, who was determined to annex Aquitaine to his realm. In 1337, the French king confiscated the remaining English

Man-at-arms wearing a felt cap and armed with a decorated war hammer.
(*Photo and copyright by Genz d'armes 1415*)

territorial possessions on the Continent and sent an army to occupy them. After a very short campaign, only Gascony remained in Edward III's hands. At this point, understanding that war with France was inevitable, King Edward refused to seek a peaceful resolution to the crisis and responded to the French moves by laying claim to the crown of France as the grandson of Charles IV. Unsurprisingly, the French nobles considered Edward's claims to be illegitimate and continued their support for Philip VI, who was the nephew of Charles IV. As a result of these events, a fresh conflict erupted between England and France, one that would end only in 1453 and thus become known as the Hundred Years' War.

Chapter 2

The First Phase of the War, 1337–1354

Both Edward III of England and Philip VI of France were ambitious kings who wanted to expand their territorial possessions and transform their realms into centralized monarchies. From a formal point of view, Edward was a vassal of Philip because of his possessions in France, and thus was required to recognize the suzerainty of the French monarch over his continental lands. Edward, however, wanted to reconquer all the French territories that had been lost by the previous Plantagenet kings (those from Henry II onwards) and planned to eliminate any residual form of influence exerted by Philip VI over the French regions that were under English control. Furthermore, King Edward was determined to claim the French crown for himself due to the realm's complex dynastic situation. When Charles IV of France died in 1328, the nearest male in line to the throne was Edward III, who had inherited his right through his mother, Isabella (who was the sister of the dead king). The French nobles, who did not want to have a foreigner as their monarch, opposed Edward III's claims by stating that Isabella could not transmit a right that she – as a woman – did not possess since only men could be kings. They decided that the nearest heir through male ancestry was Charles IV's first cousin, Philip, the Count of Valois. Count Philip, as we have seen, was crowned as Philip VI. With the ascendancy of the new monarch, the old French dynasty of the Capetians officially came to an end and the new one of the House of Valois began. Edward III, despite paying homage to Philip VI as the latter's vassal, never renounced his claims on the French throne, using them as justification for the expansionist policy that he wanted to carry on in France. By 1337, the main bone of contention between the two rival kings was Gascony, which was a key region in many aspects and formed the ancestral core of the English possessions in France. Located in south-western France, just north of the Pyrenees, it was inhabited by a population that had its own language and customs, which were quite different from those of the other French people. Gascony produced large quantities of red wine, which were shipped in a profitable trade with the English. This trade provided significant revenues to the English monarchy and was a fundamental component of the Gascon economy. Philip VI wanted to annex Gascony to his domains as soon as possible, in order to consolidate the power of his new dynasty in southern France, and was also impatient to eradicate what remained of the English presence on the Continent.

To achieve his political objectives, considering the English military capabilities to be inferior to his own, Philip VI carried on a foreign policy that was characterized by strong anti-English elements. First of all, he established a strong military alliance with the Kingdom of Scotland, which caused great concern to Edward III. Since 1332, England and Scotland had been embroiled in the Second War of Scottish Independence. The Scots, being much weaker than the English militarily and economically, were happy to obtain a strong continental ally such as France. Edward III, meanwhile, was extremely worried about a possible military collaboration between the Scots and the French, since Scotland would be able to invade northern England if most of the English troops were deployed in France to campaign against Philip VI. King Philip also carried on an anti-English foreign policy in Flanders, where the towns and cities were dependent on supplies of wool coming from England in order to produce the textile materials that they exported across most of Europe. Philip VI won the loyalty of the Flemish aristocrats and planned to annex the Flemish lands to his domains, but the local governments of the various cities sided with the English in view of a future confrontation between Philip and Edward. The French monarch assembled a large fleet at Marseilles in 1336, with the excuse of preparing a new crusading expedition to the Levant. Within a few months, however, the French armada moved to the Channel off Normandy in an obvious act of provocation against the English. There was a further French provocation during 1336 when Philip VI asked for the extradition of Robert III of Artois from English territory in Gascony. Robert, an exile from the French court who had fallen out with King Philip over an inheritance claim, became an important advisor and collaborator of Edward III, one who could be vital in the event of an English invasion of France.

When the English authorities in Gascony refused to hand over Robert of Artois, Philip VI – with the support of his major vassals – ordered the confiscation of the English territorial possessions in France. Edward III responded to this act by challenging Philip VI's rights to the French throne. Before the beginning of hostilities, the English strategy was to hold their positions in Gascony while a sizeable expeditionary force invaded France from the north. To form such an invasion force, Edward needed a large sum of money that had to be available in a very short time, so a plan was developed to make virtually all of the Kingdom of England's wool stock available to help finance the new war. A total of 30,000 sacks of wool were sold by the English merchants and the immense sum earned from this commercial operation – around £200,000 – was lent to the monarchy. Edward was also forced to borrow heavily from the great banking houses of Florence, which had collaborated with the

Man-at-arms equipped with an early form of *sallet* and armed with a poleaxe. (*Photo and copyright by Les Lions du Kent*)

Man-at-arms armed with a poleaxe. (*Photo and copyright by Alliance des Lions d'Anjou*)

Man-at-arms wearing a full set of plate armour. (*Photo and copyright by Alliance des Lions d'Anjou*)

English crown for many years. The collecting of the funds necessary to assemble an expeditionary force, however, were delayed by a series of factors, which had negative consequences for the military operations that the English were conducting in France. Consequently, within a few months, the French troops were able to occupy large parts of Gascony despite strong resistance by the local English forces. The French, who had a significant military superiority on land, were also much better prepared to act at sea than the English. Philip VI had hired a large number of warships from the Italian maritime power of Genoa, and these vessels, being manned by expert crews, were able to strike almost at will upon the English coast during 1337 and 1338. Portsmouth and Southampton, for example, were both raided and sacked. In July 1339, the French fleet in the Channel prepared a great raid on the Cinque Ports, with the objective of destroying English naval resources, but this time the English mounted an effective response, with two Plantagenet fleets commanded by Robert Morley able to intercept the French before they could strike. Surprised by the enemy, the French and Genoese warships escaped to their harbours in order to avoid a direct confrontation with the English. Soon after these events, after quarrelling over pay, the Genoese crews mutinied against the French and returned to Italy with their vessels. This was a significant blow for the French, who definitively lost their naval supremacy in the Channel.

In September 1339, Edward III was finally able to assemble an army of 12,000 men in the Low Countries, with which he advanced on French-held Cambrai. The city was besieged but not taken by the English, who then advanced into France proper. Edward's forces laid waste to a large area of French countryside, plundering and burning hundreds of villages, before the main French army moved against them. Edward, well aware of his numerical inferiority, avoided a direct confrontation with the enemy. After plundering further portions of French countryside, he marched his troops out of France without being pursued by Philip VI. The political situation in Flanders was quite delicate, the local ruler – the Count of Flanders – having remained loyal to the French king and Edward III responding by placing an embargo on all English goods that were sent to the Flemish ports. This caused the outbreak of a popular revolt in Flanders, which convinced the major cities of the region to side with England. The urban authorities of Ghent, Ypres and Bruges all recognized Edward as the legitimate King of France. By the beginning of 1340, the English defences in Gascony had been all but destroyed, but unexpected relief came for them when two of the major nobles who supported Philip VI in southern France – the Count of Armagnac and the Count of Foix – started fighting each other in a family feud. During 1340, however, the French put together a large invasion force consisting of around 400 warships that were assembled in the Zwin estuary. In order to prevent

Man-at-arms wearing a *fauld* consisting of several metal plates. (*Photo and copyright by Genz d'armes 1415*)

Man-at-arms armed with a *voulge* polearm. (*Photo and copyright by Genz d'armes 1415*)

Man-at-arms bearing an embroidered standard. (*Photo and copyright by Genz d'armes 1415*)

the French invasion of his country, Edward hastily put together a fleet in Kent. This consisted, for the major part, of deep-draught and round-hulled merchant ships known as 'cogs' that were converted for military use. In June 1340, a decisive naval clash between the French and the English took place off the port of Sluys. The English fleet tricked the French into believing that it was withdrawing, but when the wind turned in the late afternoon, the English vessels attacked with the wind behind them and destroyed most of the French warships. The Battle of Sluys was a decisive clash of the Hundred Years' War, since it gave dominance over the Channel to England for the rest of the conflict.

After triumphing at the Battle of Sluys, Edward III was able to land with a new army in northern France. He then sent part of his forces, under the command of Robert of Artois, to attack the French positions in Artois. The new land campaign, however, was a disaster for the English. The contingent commanded by Robert of Artois was almost destroyed by the French, while the main force guided by Edward failed to take the important city of Tournai after a short but costly siege. When the main French army of Philip VI arrived to confront the English, Edward III chose to avoid a pitched battle. Both sides were running out of financial resources by the autumn of 1340 and thus decided to sign a temporary truce – that lasted for nine months – on 25 September. Edward's political position was weaker than that of Philip, since most of the English nobles were against the resumption of hostilities. The English monarchy was essentially bankrupt, the activities of the English merchants having been severely damaged by the ongoing hostilities and most of Scotland having been lost due to the king's military commitment on the Continent. On 30 April 1341, however, the Duke of Brittany, John III, died without heirs. This caused the outbreak of a civil war in Brittany, which was fought between John of Montfort (half-brother of the deceased duke) and Jeanne of Penthièvre (niece of John III). According to feudal law, it was Philip VI's responsibility to decide who should inherit Brittany. The king chose Jeanne of Penthièvre, whose husband was his nephew, Charles of Blois. This decision caused the immediate rebellion of John of Montfort, who seized the Breton capital of Nantes and won the support of the population. Fearing that he would be attacked by Philip VI, John went to England to seek the support of Edward III. The English king agreed to provide help, and thus hostilities between England and France resumed. However, before any English troops could arrive in Brittany, John of Montfort was besieged by the French army in Nantes and was captured. His wife, Joanna of Flanders, continued to fight against the French troops commanded by Charles of Blois during the winter of 1341–42 until a small English expeditionary force landed at Brest. The English troops, after receiving some reinforcements, were able to reconquer most of Brittany and defeated Charles of Blois at the Battle of Morlaix on 30 September 1342. A few weeks later, Edward III landed with another English expeditionary force at Brest and started besieging Rennes. At this point, a large French army advanced into Brittany and it seemed that a large pitched battle was inevitable. Quite unexpectedly, however, a general truce was enforced when two cardinals arrived from the papal city of Avignon in January 1343. The truce lasted until 1345 and was accepted by the warring sides for different reasons. In England, the tax burden had been heavy during recent years and the debts of the Crown had become immense, while in France, Philip VI had experienced the same financial difficulties as his enemies and had been forced to introduce two new taxes. The truce left many soldiers unemployed, who rather than going back to a life of poverty decided to band together and start operating as brigands. The latter became known as '*routiers*' and represented a serious problem for some regions of France, where they looted and killed in search of supplies.

In the early months of 1345, Edward III was determined to renew full-scale war on the Continent and to attack France on three fronts: in Brittany, Gascony and Flanders. The main English expeditionary force anchored off Sluys in Flanders until 22 July, when it sailed towards Normandy. Once on the move, however, it was scattered by a storm and was forced to return home without having landed any contingent on French soil. These events greatly advantaged Philip VI, who could send some of the forces that he had assembled in northern France to the secondary fronts of Brittany and Gascony. In Gascony, the English obtained a series of significant victories, despite their numerical inferiority. They took some enemy castles by surprise, which encouraged Edward III to send more troops to southern France. On 9 August 1345, 500 men-at-arms and 1,500 archers arrived in Bordeaux, ready to attack the French. The following English offensive was a great success, leading to the defeat of a French heavy cavalry force that was ambushed by Plantagenet troops outside Bergerac. To restore his positions in Gascony, Philip VI sent his son and heir, John of Normandy, to southern France with an army of 20,000 men. John carried out an effective counter-offensive and besieged several castles that were in English hands. However, on 21 October 1345, the English attacked the French army's camp after a night march and gained an unexpected victory. The French suffered severe losses, with several of their noble commanders taken prisoner. The four-month English campaign in Gascony had been the first successful one fought by Plantagenet troops in France since the beginning of the Hundred Years' War in 1337. During the first half of 1346, King Edward gathered a new large army in England for an invasion of northern France. Since the English no longer controlled any major Flemish port, the French expected a Plantagenet landing in Brittany or Gascony. The French had already organized a major counter-offensive in Gascony and were besieging English

Man-at-arms attacking with his poleaxe. (*Photo and copyright by Les Lions du Kent*)

Man-at-arms wearing a soft cap and a full set of plate armour.
(*Photo and copyright by Les Lions du Kent*)

Heavy infantryman (left) and man-at-arms (right). The shield of the knight is of a model designed for jousting. (*Photo and copyright by Les Lions du Kent*)

troops garrisoned in the important castle of Aiguillon. Philip VI was sure that Edward would therefore direct his expeditionary force towards southern France.

Contrary to his enemies' expectations, however, the English monarch landed in northern Normandy – not far from Cherbourg – on 12 July 1346. The Plantagenet expeditionary force, numbering 10,000 men, achieved complete strategic surprise. Yet Edward III did not want to conduct a large-scale invasion of northern France, his plan being a devastating raid to significantly reduce his opponents' morale and wealth. The English army marched south through the Cotentin peninsula, cutting a wide arc of destruction through some of the richest areas of France. The Plantagenet troops burned every town they encountered along the way, while the English fleet kept pace with the land forces in order to transport vast amounts of loot. The English soldiers stormed and sacked Caen before reaching the Seine river at the beginning of August. Meanwhile, Philip VI mobilized all his forces in northern France and prepared for a long campaign. The French troops besieging Aiguillon, commanded by Philip VI's son, John, were recalled north and ordered to join the main force that was tasked with intercepting Edward III. The French started to carry out a scorched earth policy in order to slow down the movement of the English, carrying away all stores of food from the territories that were to be crossed by the enemy. The English were thus forced to spread out over a wide area to forage, which significantly slowed down their march. Philip VI reached the Somme river one day before Edward III and established his main base at Amiens, also sending large detachments to hold every bridge and ford across the Somme between Amiens and the Channel. The Plantagenet troops were thereby trapped in an area that had been stripped of food, and Edward was forced to break the French blockade of the Somme in order to save his starving troops. His supplies were running out and time was becoming a crucial factor. Against all odds, however, the English monarch was able to break the enemy defences at a tidal ford named Blanchetaque and to cross the Somme. His men could then resupply after struggling for several days, which consequently boosted their morale. At this point, despite having far fewer troops then his adversary, Edward III decided to fight a pitched battle against Philip VI and prepared a defensive position at Crécy.

The English army, which had received some reinforcements while moving across northern France, mustered around 14,000 men: 2,500 men-at-arms, 3,000 'hobelars' light cavalrymen, 5,000 longbowmen and 3,500 infantrymen. The French army was much larger than that of Edward III, mustering some 30,000 men: 8,000 men-at-arms, 6,000 crossbowmen (most of whom were Genoese mercenaries) and 16,000 infantrymen of the feudal levies. King Edward deployed his army in a carefully selected position, facing south-east on a sloping hillside that was broken by copses

Man-at-arms equipped with frog-mouthed great helm. (*Photo and copyright by Genz d'armes 1415*)

Man-at-arms wearing a headgear of the *chaperon* type. (*Photo and copyright by Les Lions du Kent*)

and terracing. The left flank of the Plantagenet line was anchored against the settlement of Wadicourt, while the right wing was protected by the village of Crécy. This made it difficult for the French to outflank the English defensive positions. Furthermore, the English had a ready line of retreat in case the French prevailed in

Man-at-arms wearing a headgear of the bycocket type. (*Photo and copyright by Genz d'armes 1415*)

the coming battle. While waiting for the arrival of the French, the English troops dug pits in front of their line and deployed the few primitive gunpowder weapons that they had with them. Edward's tactical plan was to provoke the French heavy cavalry into a frontal charge uphill against his solid infantry formations, which consisted of dismounted men-at-arms and foot soldiers who were deployed on the back of the English and Welsh longbowmen. The Plantagenet troops were divided into three main sections, or battles, which were deployed in column formation. The first battle, acting as the vanguard, was commanded by the king's son and heir, Edward, Prince of Wales. The second battle, under the orders of the Earl of Arundel, was placed in the middle, while the third battle, led by Edward III himself, acted as the reserve. Each of the three battles had dismounted men-at-arms in the centre – supported by ranks of infantrymen deployed immediately behind them – and archers on each flank, as well as in a skirmish line that was formed along the front of each battle. At the beginning of the clash, many of the longbowmen were concealed in small woods or lying down in ripe wheat. To the rear of the whole army, behind the reserve, was the English baggage train, which had been partly fortified in order to serve as a defence against any possible attack coming from the rear and as a rallying point in the event of defeat. The French army had the Genoese crossbowmen in the vanguard, followed by a large battle of mounted men-at-arms that was commanded by Philip VI's brother, Count Charles of Alençon. The first cavalry battle was followed by a second one led by Duke Rudolph of Lorraine and Count Louis of Blois. The French rearguard, under the orders of Philip VI, mostly consisted of infantrymen from the feudal levies who were to act as the reserve. Philip's tactical plan was to use the darts of his Genoese crossbowmen to soften up the English infantry before launching a decisive cavalry charge. Such a plan would have worked well if the English infantry had not included so many archers, but the French monarch had not taken into consideration the incredible firepower of the enemy longbows.

As soon as the French advanced, a sudden rainstorm broke over the field, whereupon the English archers unstrung their bows to avoid the strings becoming wet and slackened. The Genoese crossbowmen tried to take advantage of this and engaged the English longbowmen in an archery duel. The English archers, however, outranged their opponents and had a rate of fire more than three times greater. Furthermore, the Genoese crossbowmen were not protected by their usual *pavise* shields, which were still with the French baggage in the rear. The Italian mercenaries soon got into great difficulties, the mud impeding their ability to reload, which required them to press the stirrups of their crossbows into the ground. After a short duel, and having suffered significant losses, the Genoese were routed by the English longbowmen and fled the field. The French knights of the first cavalry battle hacked at the retreating mercenaries, calling them cowards and traitors. Several Italian crossbowmen were killed by the French men-at-arms in a moment of confusion that was worsened by the fire of the handful of English gunpowder weapons. At this point, the first battle of the French cavalry launched a frontal charge against the English positions. This had to force its way through the fleeing Genoese and was further slowed down by the muddy ground. While charging uphill, among the pits dug by the enemy, the French knights came under a rain of arrows fired by the English longbowmen, who preserved their ammunition until they had a reasonable chance of penetrating the cuirasses of the French men-at-arms at a range of about 80m. Hundreds of French knights were killed, but the casualties suffered by French horses were even greater, the wounded horses falling to the ground and spilling or trapping their riders. By the time a few of the surviving French knights reached the positions of the dismounted English men-at-arms, the cavalry charge had already lost most of its impetus. The English infantrymen then moved forward to kill the French wounded and loot their bodies, while the archers recovered arrows from the ground.

Philip VI, despite having seen the failure of his first assault, ordered the second cavalry battle of his army to launch another frontal charge. This had to be conducted through ground that was littered with dead men and horses. The second charge of the French knights had exactly the same result as the first one, although some more French men-at-arms reached the English line and engaged the Plantagenet dismounted knights in hand-to-hand combat. The Prince of Wales distinguished himself in this phase of the battle, which saw Edward III sending forward a detachment from his reserve in order to reinforce his son's position. After the first two charges, which ended in disaster for the French, they launched other minor assaults against the English positions until the coming of darkness. The French nobility stubbornly refused to yield and did not want to accept defeat at the hands of a bunch of commoners equipped with longbows. Philip VI was caught up in the fighting: he had two horses killed underneath him and received an arrow in the jaw. The Oriflamme, the sacred banner of the French forces, was captured by the English. After many hours of fighting and having suffered severe losses, the French finally abandoned the field. On the following day, the disorganized French feudal infantry, which had played no role in the battle, was pursued for miles and routed by the now mounted English men-at-arms. The Battle of Crécy was an enormous success for Edward III. The casualties of the Plantagenet troops were extremely low, numbering only around 300, while the French lost some 2,000 knights and 10,000 infantrymen. A disproportionate number of leading aristocrats were among the dead on the French side, including ten counts and one duke.

Following their incredible victory at Crécy, the English army marched north and continued devastating large swathes of French territory. Edward III then decided to capture the coastal city of Calais, which could act as an important English naval base. The Plantagenets needed to control a major harbour in northern France, where fresh expeditionary forces could land in the future; Calais was an obvious choice, since it

Heavy infantryman equipped with spear and rectangular shield. The helmet is covered with metal scales. (*Photo and copyright by Genz d'armes 1415*)

Heavy infantryman equipped with spear and rectangular shield. His shoulders are protected by metal scales. (*Photo and copyright by Genz d'armes 1415*)

Heavy infantryman wearing an open *bascinet*. (*Photo and copyright by Genz d'armes 1415*)

had established port facilities and was located near to the coast of south-east England. The English siege of Calais, which starting during the summer of 1345, proved to be a difficult undertaking, the city being strongly fortified and surrounded by extensive marshes. Meanwhile, after his devastating defeat at Crécy, Philip VI was obliged to rebuild his army almost from scratch. While the main English army besieged Calais, the Plantagenet forces in Gascony launched a massive raiding expedition, or *chevauchée*, through Saintonge, Aunis and Poitou. The English captured several towns and castles without being intercepted, and were even able to storm the rich city of Poitiers. With the French state on the verge of bankruptcy, Philip was unable to form a new army due to lack of funds. He could not send reinforcements to Calais and was forced to disband what remained of his troops. Hoping to gain some precious time for recovery and to reduce the Plantagenet pressure on his territories, Philip called on the Scots to fulfil their military obligations as allies of France. The Scottish King David II, convinced that the English were focused entirely on France, invaded northern England. However, he was soo defeated by a small Plantagenet force – raised exclusively from the counties of northern England – at the Battle of Neville's Cross. This battle was a disaster for the Scots, with David II being captured and several leading Scottish nobles killed. The battle was also of great strategic importance, freeing English forces for the war against France because the border counties of northern England proved able to guard against the remaining Scottish threat from their own military resources.

During 1346 and the early months of 1347, the siege of Calais continued, with the French trying to cut the English supply lines from Flanders. Yet the Plantagenet forces eventually gained the upper hand, taking control of the entrance to the harbour of Calais, which prevented the besieged troops from receiving supplies and determined the outcome of the siege. On 3 August 1347, after having run out of food, the defenders of Calais surrendered and the city was captured by Edward III. The English king soon expelled the entire French population from the city and repopulated it with English people. Calais would remain in English hands for more than two centuries and played a vital strategic role during the remainder of the Hundred Years' War as the main Plantagenet naval base in France. Following the fall of Calais, both warring sides desired to suspend hostilities in order to stabilize their financial position. Two cardinals, acting as emissaries of the Pope, found Edward III and Philip VI willing to listen to their proposals, and on 28 September 1347, the Truce of Calais was formally agreed. For the duration of the truce, the English were confirmed in possession of their territorial conquests in France. The truce was originally to run for nine months until 7 July 1348, but it was repeatedly extended over the years until 1355, mostly due to the outbreak of the devastating plague known as the Black Death.

Heavy infantryman equipped with a kettle helmet and padded *aketon*.
(*Photo and copyright by Genz d'armes 1415*)

Heavy infantryman armed with a *voulge* polearm.
(*Photo and copyright by Genz d'armes 1415*)

Heavy infantryman bearing an embroidered standard. (*Photo and copyright by Genz d'armes 1415*)

Chapter 3

The Second Phase of the War, 1355–1389

The Black Death reached England in 1348 and had a devastating effect, causing the deaths of tens of thousands of people, as had happened in countries throughout Europe. By 1355, the disease had receded sufficiently to allow the Kingdom of England to start rebuilding its finances and for Edward III to resume hostilities with France. His eldest son and successor, Edward, Prince of Wales – who was nicknamed the 'Black Prince' because of the colour of his armour – was appointed overall commander of the English forces in Gascony. Prince Edward began assembling men and supplies soon after his arrival in France, with the intention of launching offensive operations against the French. He commanded around 2,000 English soldiers, who were supported by 6,000 troops provided by the Gascon vassals of the English Crown. The Kingdom of France was now ruled by John II, who had succeeded his father after the death of Philip VI in 1350. In October 1355, the Black Prince set out on a large-scale *chevauchée*, which immediately had great success. The Anglo-Gascon raiding force marched 300 miles from Bordeaux to Narbonne, which was located almost on the Mediterranean coastline and deep in French-held territory. The Plantagenet troops devastated a wide swathe of enemy territory and sacked many French cities on the way. The French forces facing them preferred to avoid any direct confrontation, so there was little proper fighting. The Black Prince's expedition nevertheless caused enormous economic damage to France, while also revealing to the major French nobles the military weakness of their monarch. A series of offensive actions were carried out in 1356 by the English troops, who captured some fifty enemy towns and fortifications in a period of just four months. The English victories convinced many French nobles whose territories were located on the borders of Gascony to side with the Plantagenets, which drastically weakened the position of John II in southern France. The new heavy taxes imposed by the French monarchy were hated by a large portion of the French population, causing the spread of malcontent. There was, for instance, a major rebellion in the city of Arras, and the leading nobles of Normandy refused to pay taxes to their king. Thereafter, sensing an opportunity, Edward III diverted an expedition planned for Brittany to Normandy. Around 2,300 English soldiers, under the command of Henry of Lancaster, landed in Normandy and started pillaging their way westward across the Norman countryside.

Heavy infantryman wearing a padded *aketon* over his cuirass of mail armour.
(*Photo and copyright by Genz d'armes 1415*)

Heavy infantryman equipped with an open *bascinet*. (*Photo and copyright by Genz d'armes 1415*)

The Second Phase of the War, 1355–1389

Heavy infantryman equipped with a kettle helmet. (*Photo and copyright by Genz d'armes 1415*)

John II, hoping to obtain the first significant victory of his reign, mobilized a large army and moved to Rouen in order to intercept the Plantagenet forces. The French monarch started to pursue the English troops, but bungled several opportunities to bring his enemies to battle, allowing them to escape.

On 4 August 1356, the English forces in Gascony launched another raiding expedition, this time heading north from Bergerac. The Black Prince separated his forces into three divisions, which moved north abreast of each other and began to systematically devastate the French countryside. The three English contingents operated autonomously but were able to join forces at a day's notice in case of an enemy counter-offensive. The advance of Prince Edward was deliberately destructive and brutal; it had a methodical nature and was aimed at causing serious damage to the French economy. The resistance of the French was quite weak because the best troops of John II were still deployed in Normandy to counter the activities of Henry of Lancaster. In late August 1356, however, the French monarch finally decided to march against the Black Prince at the head of his main army. Prince Edward, upon learning of the French king's movements, brought together his three raiding divisions and moved towards the Loire river. He probably hoped to link up with the English forces in Normandy after having fought a pitched battle with the French. John II, in preparation for a confrontation with the Black Prince, sent home nearly all of his infantry contingents and reorganized his army as an entirely mounted force. The French now had the mobility and speed that were needed to match Prince Edward's all-mounted raiding force. On 8 September, the English army reached Tours, where the Black Prince prepared his men for battle. The Plantagenet commander hoped to receive some reinforcements from Henry of Lancaster, but the unusual height of the Loire river and the French control of its bridges prevented the English troops in the north from joining those from Gascony.

After failed peace negotiations, both the English and French armies resumed their march in search of a suitable battlefield. John II's troops moved south parallel to the English in an attempt to cut their lines of retreat and supply. An initial skirmish between the French and Plantagenet forces happened on 17 September, which convinced King John to draw up his army outside Poitiers in battle formation. On 18 September, the Anglo-Gascon troops also reached Poitiers and prepared for a pitched clash. As had happened several years before at Crécy, the English created some very strong defensive positions on the battlefield by digging pits and trenches, also erecting barricades in front of their lines with the intention of repulsing the attacks of the enemy cavalry. While both armies completed their preparations, there were further peace talks but these had no significant results. Although John II was not completely convinced about the idea of attacking the English, his headstrong nobles were eager to avenge the devastation committed by the Plantagenet raiders on French soil. Meanwhile, the Black Prince's army was running out of supplies and could only have survived if the outcome of the impending battle was in their favour. The Anglo-Gascon army numbered around 6,000 men: 3,000 men-at-arms, 2,000 English-Welsh longbowmen and 1,000 Gascon light infantrymen (known as 'bidowers'). According to contemporary sources, only some 1,000 of the men-at-arms came from England, while the remaining 2,000 were Gascons. While all the Anglo-Gascon soldiers had travelled on horse across France, they were used to fighting on foot during major battles. The Black Prince's forces were divided into three divisions, or battles, as was customary for the time. The three Anglo-Gascon battles each comprised 1,000 men-at-arms and 1,000 archers, with the left commanded by the Earl of Warwick, the right led by the Earl of Salisbury and the centre under the orders of Prince Edward. The French army of John II mustered around 14,000 soldiers: 10,000 men-at-arms, 2,000 crossbowmen and 2,000 infantrymen. Differently from what happened at Crécy, the French knights at Poitiers dismounted to fight (except for two small groups). The French troops were divided into four battles: the first division consisted of 1,000 men-at-arms as well as of most of the crossbowmen and infantrymen, with the second division comprising 4,000 men-at-arms, the third division a further 3,000 men-at-arms and the fourth division the remaining 2,000 men-at-arms.

On 19 September, just after dawn, the French drew themselves up in battle order, with their leading division about 500m from the English positions. The clash began, as planned by the Black Prince, with a French attack against both the Plantagenet left and right wings. This first French assault was conducted by the few men-at-arms who were mounted, with the support of the crossbowmen. John II wanted to destroy the English and Welsh archers as soon as possible, but the marshy terrain and the arrows fired by the enemy longbowmen prevented his forces from reaching their objective. The French crossbowmen suffered heavy losses, while the heavily armoured knights were slowed down by the terrain before being attacked on the flanks by the enemy archers. The French attack on the English left was a complete failure, but that on the right was conducted more cautiously. On the right of the English line, the soldiers of the Earl of Salisbury defended a thick hedge that had a single passable gap, which was wide enough for four horses abreast. The French attempted to smash through the Plantagenet men-at-arms defending the gap, but came under intense fire from the English archers positioned in the trenches located near to the hedge. The hand-to-hand fighting between French and English dismounted knights was very intense in this sector of the front, but the attackers were ultimately repulsed with many killed or badly wounded. The failure of the initial French attack had caused the almost complete destruction of John II's first division, but the French monarch remained determined to defeat the English and soon ordered a second

Burgundian heavy infantryman wearing a *sallet*. (*Photo and copyright by Genz d'ordennance*)

Burgundian heavy infantryman wearing a *sallet*. (*Photo and copyright by Genz d'ordennance*)

Heavy infantryman wearing a breastplate of plate armour. (*Photo and copyright by Alsatiae Protectores*)

assault. This attack was conducted by the 4,000 men-at-arms of the second battle of the French army. The advancing French came under a heavy rain of English arrows and was further disordered by the retreating soldiers who had conducted the first charge. Despite suffering many losses, the attackers closed with the Plantagenet troops and fierce hand-to-hand fighting erupted. This went on for almost two hours, with the French massing against two gaps in the enemy-held hedge. At one point it seemed that the attackers were going to break through the Plantagenet line, but the precise fire of the English longbowmen stopped the French advance. Throughout the fighting, the experienced Black Prince was able to manoeuvre and redeploy his troops in order to reinforce the sectors of his line that were coming under enemy pressure. He also directed the fire of the archers where it was needed, which denied the French any chance of success. As the second French attack went on, Prince Edward was forced to commit almost all of his reserves to reinforce the weak spots of his line, but the French soldiers of the second division finally disengaged and returned to their starting positions in good order. As had happened after the first attack, the Anglo-Gascon troops did not pursue the defeated enemies: they stood their ground, tended their wounded, finished off any enemy wounded and stripped the French dead. The longbowmen, meanwhile, recovered what arrows they could find on the battlefield.

Following the failure of their second attack, many of the French abandoned the battlefield. The survivors of the first and second divisions took no further part in the fighting and fled, together with a portion of the third division. Only 1,600 men-at-arms from the third French battle remained on the field and joined forces with the fourth battle , which was commanded by John II. The French king, despite having already lost a large part of his army, ordered the Oriflamme to be unfurled – which signalled that no prisoners were to be taken – and launched a last desperate charge at the head of his best knights. The Black Prince harangued his exhausted men in an attempt to stiffen their morale, but he quickly realized that his troops were in no condition to repulse another enemy assault. Consequently, he attempted a cunning stratagem, sending a small mounted force of Gascons on a circuitous march around the French flank to launch a surprise attack on their rear. At the same time, Prince Edward ordered a general advance of all his forces, which bolstered Anglo-Gascon morale and took the French by surprise. The archers advanced ahead of the English forces and engaged the enemy crossbowmen, who were supporting the French knights of King John. Despite running out of arrows, the longbowmen were victorious in the confrontation with the French crossbowmen and routed them. Soon after this, the English and French men-at-arms came into contact and the decisive melee of the battle started. The Anglo-Welsh archers, who had already used all their arrows, threw their longbows aside and joined the Plantagenet knights in the hand-to-hand fighting. The fighting was furious and the clash appeared to be in the balance for some time until the appearance of the 160 mounted Gascons that the Black Prince had sent against the enemy rear. These launched a surprise charge against the back of the French formation, killing a significant number of men. Exhausted and now surrounded, the French forces gradually lost cohesion and started to flee from the battlefield in complete disorder. The few French soldiers who continued to fight were surrounded and split into small groups. Their position was clearly hopeless and the English were eager to take them prisoner in order that they could be ransomed. The sacred Oriflamme banner was captured by the Plantagenet troops, together with John II and his sons Louis and Philip. The French monarch had continued to fight with his personal bodyguards until he was completely surrounded by a large number of enemies. The fleeing French soldiers tried to reach Poitiers in search of safety, but the inhabitants of the city – fearing an English reaction – closed the gates of their walls and refused access to the defeated troops. The mounted English knights who pursued the French caught up with them as they milled outside the gates, and many were killed. The Battle of Poitiers was the most devastating defeat suffered by the French during the Hundred Years' War. Approximately 2,500 of their men-at-arms were killed, together with 3,000 infantrymen and crossbowmen. The English captured around 2,500 enemy knights and 500 infantrymen/crossbowmen. The King of France was now a prisoner of Edward III, together with his sons Louis and Philip and many of the most powerful French aristocrats. The losses suffered by the Black Prince's army were not particularly significant, probably numbering around 600 men.

Following his great victory at the Battle of Poitiers, Prince Edward went back with his army and his many prisoners to Gascony, where he made a triumphal entrance into the city of Bordeaux. Now that John II had been captured by the Plantagenets, any form of central authority existing in France dissolved into near anarchy. In March 1357, a truce was agreed for two years between the two warring sides, and several weeks later the Black Prince landed at Plymouth with John II. The French king was obliged to undertake protracted negotiations with his rival, Edward III, which culminated in the signing of the First Treaty of London in May 1358. According to the terms of the treaty, the French ceded large sections of territory to the English and agreed to pay a substantial ransom for John's freedom. The leading French nobles, however, were unenthusiastic about the terms prescribed by the treaty and were unable to raise the first instalment of the ransom from their domains. Consequently, the treaty soon lapsed and hostilities with England resumed, while a major peasant revolt, or *jacquerie*, broke out in northern France. John II was then forced to sign the Second Treaty of London, which was similar to the first except that even larger swathes of French territory were to be transferred to the Plantagenets. In May 1359,

Heavy infantryman wearing a kettle helmet. (*Photo and copyright by Alsatiae Protectores*)

Heavy infantryman wearing a *sallet*. (*Photo and copyright by Genz d'ordennance*)

Heavy infantryman armed with a bill polearm and war hammer. (*Photo and copyright by Alliance des Lions d'Anjou*)

the terms of the new treaty were rejected by Charles, the son of John II, and the major nobles of France. The war thus continued, and Edward III landed at Calais at the head of a large expeditionary force on 28 October 1359. The English troops marched through Artois and Cambresis to Rheims, where Edward intended to be crowned King of France. The Plantagenets began besieging Rheims, but the city – where all the French monarchs had been crowned for centuries – had strong defences. After failing to take Rheims, the English king broke up the siege in early 1360 and led his army into Burgundy, where he could resupply his troops. In April, the English marched towards the Loire river and went back to their starting positions, having failed to fight a major pitched battle against the French. At this point, both the English and the French had consumed most of their financial resources and were in no condition to continue hostilities. As a result, new peace negotiations started between the Black Prince and the Dauphin of France, Charles (the first son and designated successor of John II). On 8 May 1360, the Treaty of Brétigny was signed, according to which a full third of France was to be ceded to the English and John II had to be ransomed for 3 million gold *écus*. The following French territories were obtained by Edward III, in addition to those he already possessed in Gascony: Poitou, Saintonge, Aunis, Agenais, Périgord, Limousin, Quercy, Bigorre, Guaré, Angoumois, Rouergue, Montreuil-sur-Mer, Pomthieu, Calais, Sangatte, Ham and Guines. The King of England was to hold all these areas, without having to pay feudal homage for them. As a guarantee for the payment of his ransom, John II gave as hostages two of his sons: Louis I, Duke of Anjou, and John, Duke of Berry. In return for all this, Edward III formally renounced all his claims on the French throne.

In 1362, Louis of Anjou escaped captivity while his father was still putting together the money needed to pay his ransom, after which John II felt honour-bound to return to captivity in England. This greatly weakened the political position of the French crown, to the advantage of King John's various enemies. The Kingdom of Navarre, located in northern Spain and south of Gascony, used the captivity of the French monarch in London to attack France during 1363. The Navarrese could count on the unofficial support of Edward III and thus hoped to conquer large parts of southern France for themselves now that the French military forces were in a state of complete chaos. In 1364, John II died in England while still in honourable captivity. He was succeeded by the Dauphin of France, who became monarch as Charles V. On 16 May 1364, a month after the French king's accession, the Battle of Cocherel was fought between France and Navarre. The clash, against all odds, ended in a significant victory for the French, who crushed the Navarrese forces. The Battle of Cocherel was important for three reasons: first, it caused the defeat of the Kingdom of Navarre in the ongoing conflict; second, it was the first occasion in which an important French

Heavy infantryman equipped with *sallet* and short-sleeved corselet of mail armour. (*Photo and copyright by Genz d'ordennance*)

Heavy infantryman with an open *bascinet* and padded *aketon*.
(*Photo and copyright by Genz d'armes 1415*)

Heavy infantryman armed with a massive war hammer and wearing a kettle helmet. (*Photo and copyright by Alliance des Lions d'Anjou*)

military commander – Bertrand du Guesclin – distinguished himself; and third, it was also the first occasion in which a force of English longbowmen (300 of them, fighting as mercenaries for the Navarrese) was defeated on the open field by the French. While these events took place in southern France, a new civil war broke out in Brittany between John of Montfort and Charles of Blois, who – as we have seen – had already fought against each other for possession of the Breton lands some decades before. John of Montfort was supported by England, while Charles of Blois had the backing of France and the Breton warlord Bertrand du Guesclin. Initially, Charles of Blois obtained a series of minor victories, but John of Montfort gradually gained the upper hand. On 29 September 1364, the decisive Battle of Auray was fought between the rival aristocrats. The clash was a disaster for the pro-French faction, with Charles of Blois being killed and Bertrand du Guesclin captured. The Breton warlord was later ransomed by Charles V for 100,000 francs, but Brittany definitively came under the control of John of Montfort. The support given by the English to John of Montfort during the Breton civil war produced no significant benefits for Edward III, who no longer had a claim to the throne of France, and thus John of Montfort had to accept the suzerainty of Charles V in order to hold the Duchy of Brittany in peace. The French, however, benefited through the improved generalship of Bertrand du Guesclin, who left Brittany and entered the service of Charles V. After the restoration of peace on French soil, many French soldiers and mercenaries became unemployed and turned to plundering. This soon became a serious problem for the King of France, who tried to find employment outside the boundaries of his kingdom for the many veterans who ravaged the countryside to eke out a living.

Charles V found the opportunity to do so when a civil war broke out in the Kingdom of Castile, the most powerful realm of Spain which had been ruled by Peter the Cruel since 1350. Peter had married the sister-in-law of Charles V, but instead of being a loyal ally of France he had sided with the Navarrese when they invaded the southern territories of France. Peter was a very ambitious monarch who wanted to expand his kingdom as much as possible. He initiated hostilities with the Kingdom of Aragon in 1356 with the aim of conquering the area, and in 1362 concluded a strong military alliance with the Black Prince after having poisoned his French wife. The French responded to these acts by allying themselves with the Aragonese and sponsoring the outbreak of a civil war in the Kingdom of Castile. The Castilian nobles hated Peter the Cruel because of his despotism and opposed the continuation of the war with Aragon. In 1366, the Castilian Civil War broke out when the illegitimate brother of Peter – Henry – decided to claim the throne of Castile for himself. Henry was supported by the leading aristocracy of Castile, as well as by France, Aragon and the papacy. Charles V ordered Bertrand du Guesclin to lend

Heavy infantryman armed with a sword and wearing a kettle helmet. (*Photo and copyright by Alsatiae Protectores*)

Heavy infantryman equipped with an early form of *sallet*.
(*Photo and copyright by Genz d'ordennance*)

Heavy infantryman equipped with a sword and small round shield of the buckler type. (*Photo and copyright by Les Lions du Kent*)

the bands of unemployed French soldiers to Henry, who was thus able to assemble a large army at Montpellier with which he invaded Castile and deposed Peter. Fleeing to Bayonne in English-held Gascony, Peter petitioned his ally Prince Edward for aid in exchange for lands in Castile. The Black Prince accepted and marched into Castile, where the decisive Battle of Navarrete was fought on 3 April 1367. This saw a confrontation between Peter and Henry but also between Prince Edward and Bertrand du Guesclin, who were present on the battlefield. Peter commanded around 10,000 men, comprising the following elements 8,400 mercenaries mostly hailing from the English territorial possessions in France, 500 English longbowmen, 800 Castilians and 300 Navarrese. Henry was in clear numerical inferiority, who had just 1,000 French mercenaries, 2,500 Castilians and 1,000 Aragonese. At the beginning of the battle, Bertrand du Guesclin charged at the head of his French mercenaries, but the Gascon mercenaries of the Black Prince soon started to outflank him. The fire of the English archers prevented the Castilians from moving to support the French, and after Bertrand du Guesclin was completely surrounded, the army of Henry fled from the field. Despite being a clear victory for him, the Battle of Navarrete did not have positive consequences for the Black Prince: Henry managed to escape to France and continued his struggle, while Peter the Cruel did not reimburse the huge sum of money that had been needed to hire the Anglo-Gascon mercenaries and did not cede to the English the Castilian territories that had been agreed some time before. Shortly after the Battle of Navarrete, the Anglo-Castilian alliance broke up. Two years later, in 1369, Henry conquered the Kingdom of Castile after having defeated and killed Peter at the Battle of Montiel. Having been crowned with the decisive support of France, Henry became the most loyal and precious ally of the French. Due to the location of their kingdom, the Castilians could attack Gascony from the south. They also lent a large fleet in the Bay of Biscay to the French in return for the military aid that they had received from Charles V. During the 1370s, the Castilian corsairs raided the southern coast of England with relative impunity, while the Black Prince tried to recover his enormous economic losses by raising new taxes in his French domains. This caused great malcontent among the Gascons, who – for the first time – started to resent English rule. Charles V summoned Prince Edward to answer the complaints of his Gascon vassals, but the Black Prince refused.

France resumed hostilities against England in 1369. The balance of power had now shifted in favour of Charles V, as England had lost its most capable military leaders: Edward III was too old and the Black Prince had started to suffer from serious health problems. Bertrand du Guesclin, meanwhile, was appointed Constable of France, with overall command of the French forces, in November 1370. The experienced Breton warlord, rather than seeking battle, adopted a strategy of attrition against the English. By conducting various small-scale campaigns that lasted for only short periods, he retook piece by piece several territories that had been lost by the French during the previous decades. The English responded by conducting a series of destructive raiding expeditions, hoping that these could bring Bertrand du Guesclin to battle. In 1369 and 1375 there were two outbreaks of the Black Death, which had a devastating impact on Gascony. In 1372, the Battle of La Rochelle took place at sea. A Castilian fleet of twenty-two warships decisively defeated an English fleet of thirty-two vessels, with the entire Plantagenet naval force being destroyed or captured. The defeat undermined English seaborne trade and supplies through the Channel, which also badly damaged the economy of Gascony. After the Battle of La Rochelle, the English raiding operations conducted on land lost most of their previous importance, the French having learned how to counter them in an effective way. A large-scale English *chevauchée* in 1373 ended in complete failure when the French intercepted the Plantagenet baggage train while it was crossing the Loire river. By the time the English soldiers reached Bordeaux, they had been decimated by disease and starvation. Following these events, under the instigation of the papacy, England and France signed the Treaty of Bruges in 1375 and agreed a truce of twelve months. On 8 June 1376, the Black Prince died, followed by his father, Edward III, on 21 June 1377. The Black Prince's second son, who was still a child at that time, became the new King of England as Richard II. In 1380, the English conducted a new *chevauchée* in Brittany and laid siege to Nantes, but during 1381 they were forced to suspend their operations without having achieved any significant result. Meanwhile, in 1380, the French had also lost their monarch Charles V and Bertrand du Guesclin. This caused serious problems of leadership in France, since the son and successor of Charles V, Charles VI, was just a child. He was placed under a regency led by his uncles, who managed to maintain an effective grip on government affairs until 1388. The regents attempted to reimpose some taxes that had been cancelled by Charles V, but this led to the outbreak of violent popular revolts in several French cities, including Paris. By 1389, the war's pace had largely slowed down, with both England and France finding themselves unable to organize further military campaigns. From 1383–85, England and France fought a sort of 'proxy war' in the Iberian Peninsula, where forces of the Kingdom of Castile invaded the Kingdom of Portugal. The English supported the Portuguese, while the French backed their loyal Castilian allies. The conflict ended with victory for Portugal but had little practical consequence for the course of the Hundred Years' War. On 18 July 1389, the Truce of Leulinghem was signed between England and France, which was to last for twenty-seven years. Both countries were experiencing serious financial and internal problems, so were in no condition to continue the conflict.

Heavy infantrymen wearing different versions of *sallet* helmet.
(*Photo and copyright by Genz d'ordennance*)

Heavy infantrymen wearing a breastplate over a long-sleeved corselet of mail armour. (*Photo and copyright by Genz d'ordennance*)

The Second Phase of the War, 1355–1389

Heavy infantrymen wearing a *sallet* helmet and breastplate.
(*Photo and copyright by Genz d'ordennance*)

Chapter 4

The Third Phase of the War, 1390–1428

During the 1390s, the prospect of resuming hostilities with France became increasingly unpopular in England, mostly due to the high taxes needed for the war effort. The new monarch, Richard II, was very young and inexperienced, having no interest in expanding his territorial domains as had his more warlike predecessors. Richard ruled with the support of a small group of close friends and advisors, who – by influencing the decisions of the monarch – pursued their own personal interests rather than trying to resolve the many problems experienced by their English subjects. This caused widespread malcontent in the realm, especially among the peasant communities and the most important feudal lords. These nobles formed a strong political group, known as the Lords Appellant, which managed to press charges of treason against five of Richard II's closest friends and advisors. The Lords Appellant were in favour of resuming hostilities with France, but after becoming the leading political group of England they were not able to raise the funds that were needed to organize a new military campaign on the Continent. Over time, Richard II gradually rebuilt his personal power, thanks in part to the support of his uncle, John of Gaunt. In 1397, the king finally reasserted his authority over the Lords Appellant and destroyed their political power. Two years later, however, John of Gaunt died and Richard made a serious mistake by deciding to disinherit his powerful uncle's son, Henry of Bolingbroke. Richard II wanted to free himself of any external influence in ruling over his kingdom, but he was not strong enough among his own vassals and did not have great popularity among the commoners. As a result, while Richard II was conducting a secondary military campaign in Ireland, Henry of Bolingbroke landed in England with his supporters and – after some minor skirmishes – deposed Richard with the support of several powerful nobles. It is believed that Richard was starved to death in captivity in 1400, but mystery still surrounds details of his demise.

Henry had himself crowned Henry IV and became the first monarch of the new House of Lancaster (which can be considered a cadet branch of the House of Plantagenet), but his reign was characterized from the beginning by significant internal and external problems. Hoping to take advantage of the political changes taking place in England, the Scots launched a series of raids against the English northern counties, while in Wales, a major uprising broke out under the guidance

Heavy infantryman equipped with a painted kettle helmet.
(*Photo and copyright by La Guerre des Couronnes*)

Heavy infantryman wearing a *sallet* helmet and a metal gorget for protection of the neck. (*Photo and copyright by Les Lions du Kent*)

Heavy infantryman wearing a helmet of the great *sallet* type and armed with a *voulge* polearm. (*Photo and copyright by Les Lions du Kent*)

of Owain Glyndŵr. Coming from a noble Welsh family with a long history, Owain soon showed himself to have exceptional politico-military abilities. While Henry IV was dealing with the Scots in the north of his kingdom, Owain was declared Prince of Wales by his supporters during 1400 and was able to free most of the Welsh territories of the English presence. Initially, the Welsh leader conducted a guerrilla-type war against the superior English forces, using the unrivalled combat ability of his longbowmen. However, his forces eventually became large enough to fight and win pitched battles against the English. Henry IV was able to stop the Scottish incursions in the north by defeating the Scots at the Battle of Homildon Hill in 1402, but could do very little to counter the Welsh rebellion because he also had to face a major feudal uprising in northern England that was led by the Earl of Northumberland. Henry IV retook control of the northern territories of his realm only in 1408. Meanwhile, in Wales, Owain Glyndŵr formed a military alliance with the French and the Castilians in 1405. The French sent some expeditionary forces to support the Welsh and the joint Franco-Welsh troops advanced as far as Worcester, obtaining a series of victories over their opponents. The Castilians, instead, used their galleys to raid and burn all the way from Cornwall to Southampton. By 1406, it seemed that Wales, having been conquered more than a century before by Edward I, was going to become an independent nation. Over time, however, the military situation improved for the English: the rebellion led by the Earl of Northumberland – who had allied himself with the Welsh – was crushed and the French stopped directly supporting Owain Glyndŵr due to their own internal problems. As a result, starting from 1409, English troops gradually regained the upper hand in Wales. Henry IV died in 1413 and was succeeded by his son, Henry V, who adopted a more conciliatory attitude to the Welsh. Royal pardons were offered to the major leaders of the rebellion, who decided to surrender, and most of Wales had been pacified by 1415. Owain Glyndŵr was never captured by his enemies and probably died around 1420, having by then become an isolated guerrilla leader.

While these events took place in the British Isles, the Kingdom of France started to be ruled by a regency because Charles VI suddenly descended into madness in 1392. The regency was dominated by the king's uncle, Philip the Bold (Duke of Burgundy), and the king's brother, Louis of Valois (Duke of Orléans). The supporters of Philip the Bold and Louis of Valois gradually organized themselves into political factions that had contrasting interests: the Burgundians and the Armagnacs (the latter taking their name from the County of Armagnac, which always supported the cause of the Duke of Orléans). The Burgundians were in favour of establishing positive diplomatic relations with England, since the Duke of Burgundy had the County of Flanders among his vast domains and the Flemish cloth merchants represented the main market for English wool on the Continent. The Armagnacs, instead, were in favour of continuing the war with England in order to recover the French territories that were still under English control. Upon the death of Philip the Bold, his son and successor, John the Fearless, became the new leader of the Burgundians. The new Duke of Burgundy had ambitions to expand his domains as much as possible, which only worsened the political situation in France. From 1402, Louis of Valois started purchasing lands and strongholds in eastern France in order to limit the expansion of the Burgundians. Having increased his personal power, the Duke of Orléans ousted John the Fearless from the council of regency. This exacerbated tensions, Louis of Valois being hated by most of the emerging French middle classes because of his anti-English attitude and his expensive lifestyle, which was financed by money derived from royal taxation.

On 23 November 1407, John the Fearless had Louis of Valois murdered in Paris, an event which marked the beginning of an outright civil war between the Burgundians and the Armagnacs. Intending to avenge his father, Charles of Orléans (the son of Louis) established a strong alliance with the Count of Armagnac by marrying his daughter and formed a large coalition of major nobles with the objective of defeating John the Fearless. The Count of Armagnac, Bernard VII, in order to fight against the Burgundians, recruited the Écorcheurs, or Flayers, mercenaries from the central regions of France who had organized themselves into violent and effective warbands. At the head of his mercenaries, Bernard VII obtained a series of victories

The full panoply of a Welsh longbowman from the 1330s. (*Photo and copyright by Toxophilus.net*)

Welsh longbowman from the 1330s armed with a falchion.
(*Photo and copyright by Toxophilus.net*)

Welsh longbowman from the 1330s preparing his bow.
(*Photo and copyright by Toxophilus.net*)

and threatened the city of Paris, whose inhabitants supported the Burgundian faction. In October 1411, however, the Duke of Burgundy entered the French capital at the head of a powerful army numbering 60,000 men. The Burgundians rapidly assumed control over most of northern France and attacked Brittany, whose feudal lord had sided with the Armagnacs. John the Fearless decisively defeated the enemy mercenaries and forced the Armagnac faction to sign a temporary truce. Since 1410, the English had taken advantage of the complex politico-military events taking place in France by supporting both the warring parties. Indeed, England could only benefit from the prosecution of the ongoing French civil war. In 1414, after hostilities resumed, Paris was retaken by the Armagnacs, after which the Duke of Burgundy sent his ambassadors to the court of Henry V in England in order to establish a solid military alliance. The English monarch, sensing a great opportunity, renewed hostilities with the Kingdom of France in 1415, thereby initiating a new phase in the Hundred Years' War.

Henry V invaded France after some failed negotiations with the Armagnacs and after having claimed for himself the title of King of France through his great-grandfather, Edward III. He landed in northern France on 13 August 1415 at the head of 12,000 soldiers and soon started besieging the port of Harfleur. The siege took longer than expected, but the French town finally surrendered on 22 September. The English suffered significant losses during this first phase of the campaign, mostly through disease, but rather than going back to England for the winter, they marched through Normandy and reached Calais, the main English stronghold in northern France. While the English campaigned in Normandy, the Armagnac French assembled an army around Rouen and moved to block the English along the Somme river. Initially, these French tactics were successful, but after a few days Henry V was finally able to cross the Somme at two fords located south of Péronne. The French wanted to avoid a pitched battle with the invaders, since they knew that the Burgundians could soon join the English. However, King Henry wanted to fight as soon as possible because his men were running out of food and had marched 260 miles in less than three weeks. Since the siege of Harfleur, the English troops had been suffering from sickness, including dysentery, so their morale was not particularly high. Henry V was greatly outnumbered by his enemies, who were now blocking his way to the safety of Calais. Delaying battle would have only weakened his tired forces and allowed the arrival of substantial French reinforcements. For the moment, the Burgundians had decided to remain neutral, as they were not sure about the possibility of an English victory. As a result, the English could not count on the arrival of any French allies.

The decisive clash of the campaign was finally fought near the village of Azincourt on 25 October 1415. The battlefield consisted of a narrow strip of open land that was located between the woods of Tramecourt and Azincourt. The English army commanded by King Henry V comprised 1,500 men-at-arms and 7,000 longbowmen, who were deployed in three divisions or battles: the right wing was commanded by the Duke of York, the left wing by Thomas Camoys and the centre by Henry himself. The veteran longbowmen were deployed at the front of the three divisions and on the flanks of the English army, where the archers could establish their positions in the woods of Tramecourt and Azincourt. The men-at-arms, all dismounted, were deployed behind the archers. As usual for the English during the Hundred Years' War, the longbowmen drove pointed wooden stakes and palings into the ground ahead of their positions in order to create a barrier to hamper the movements of the enemy cavalry. The French forces that fought at the Battle of Azincourt consisted of 15,000 men, 10,000 of whom were heavily equipped knights, the remaining 5,000 soldiers being crossbowmen, *pavisier* shield-bearers and infantrymen. The French grouped their troops into five divisions: a vanguard consisting of 4,800 men-at-arms, a central battle of 3,000 men-at-arms, a right flank with 600 men-at-arms, a left flank with 600 men-at-arms and a reserve of 1,000 men-at-arms. All the French knights were dismounted, except for those of the vanguard and the 1,000 men of the reserve who would be tasked with attacking the English rear in case of success. The 5,000 foot soldiers were all deployed as the French rearguard, the aristocrats commanding the French troops at Azincourt regarding them as unnecessary troops for the coming battle. The recently ploughed terrain of the battlefield, hemmed in by dense woodland, greatly favoured the defensive approach of the English because of its narrowness and the thick mud through which the French knights would have to move. For three hours after sunrise there was no fighting. Then the knights of the French vanguard division launched a frontal assault, having been provoked by the fire of the English longbowmen. The attacking men-at-arms were unable to outflank the positions of the enemy archers because of the encroaching woodland and could not charge through the array of sharpened stakes that protected the enemy longbowmen. As a result, they came under a rain of English arrows and suffered severe casualties before they could reach the enemy lines. After their first attack was stopped with relative ease by the English, the French commanders decided to launch a second assault with their central battle. Once again, the attacking men-at-arms came under the deadly fire of the longbowmen deployed in the woods, who continued to shoot at point-blank range. When the English archers ran out of arrows, having already killed substantial numbers of their enemy, they dropped their bows and attacked the now disordered and fatigued French with hatchets and mallets. The French knights,

The full panoply of an English longbowman from the 1340s. (*Photo and copyright by Toxophilus.net*)

many of whom had already been wounded or been blocked by the mud, could not defend themselves from the lightly equipped assailants who joined King Henry's men-at-arms. With the battlefield being so narrow, the massed French ranks were forced to fight over and on the bodies of their comrades who had fallen before them. The two flank divisions of the French also joined the second charge, which turned into a disaster for the attackers when they were surrounded by the English archers. Thousands of French men-at-arms were killed or taken prisoner during three hours of desperate fighting. Henry V distinguished himself during the most violent phase of the clash, receiving an axe blow to the head. After seeing that four of their army's divisions had been routed, the soldiers of the French reserve and the foot troops of the rearguard wisely decided to flee from the battlefield in order to avoid destruction.

The Battle of Azincourt was a catastrophic defeat for the French, who had 5,500 men-at-arms killed and another 1,500 captured. The French dead included around 100 major feudal lords, among them three dukes and nine counts. Entire aristocratic families were wiped out in the male line, and in some regions of France a whole generation of landed nobility disappeared. The French prisoners included two dukes and four counts, who were key supporters of the Armagnacs. The English demanded extremely high ransoms for the liberation of these enemy aristocrats, which had positive consequences for the finances of Henry V's kingdom. The losses suffered by King Henry's army were very low, amounting to around 600 men. Following his

English longbowman from the 1340s wearing a *bascinet* and *camail* of mail armour. (*Photo and copyright by Toxophilus.net*)

English longbowman from the 1340s wearing a padded *aketon*.
(*Photo by The Free Company of Aquitaine, copyright by Nic Hawkins*)

Frontal view of an English longbowman from the 1340s.
(*Photo by The Free Company of Aquitaine, copyright by Nic Hawkins*)

Rear view of an English longbowman from the 1340s. (*Photo by The Free Company of Aquitaine, copyright by Nic Hawkins*)

English longbowman from the 1340s; the red cross applied on the *aketon* was the distinctive symbol of the English troops (the French had a white cross). (*Photo by The Free Company of Aquitaine, copyright by Nic Hawkins*)

victory at Azincourt, Henry V rapidly returned to England in order to be received in triumph in London on 23 November. The Lancastrian monarch wanted to prepare a further invasion of northern France as soon as possible, since the bulk of his enemy's forces had been destroyed. To raise a new and larger army, however, he needed time and funds. Meanwhile, in France, the Burgundians gained the upper hand in their confrontation with the Armagnacs, who had been almost wiped out by the English and carried the blame for the defeat of Azincourt.

The year 1416 saw several important military actions taking place at sea, with a French-Genoese fleet surrounding the harbour of Harfleur and besieging the local English garrison. In August, Henry V sent his brother, the Duke of Bedford, to Harfleur at the head of a fleet. The English and the French-Genoese warships clashed at the Battle of the Seine, which ended after seven hours of bitter fighting with a decisive English victory. Harfleur was thus relieved from the French siege and England retook control of the Channel. In 1417, after almost two years of patient preparation, Henry V returned to France at the head of his troops. Taking advantage of his enemies' complete military weakness, he took Caen and conquered a large portion of Normandy. The English then started besieging Rouen, which fell in January 1419 after most of its defenders and inhabitants had died of starvation. Meanwhile, during May and June 1418, Burgundian troops had occupied Paris and the most important Armagnac leaders had been slaughtered by a mob. As a consequence, during late 1419, both Henry V of England and the Dauphin of France, Charles, tried to ally themselves with the Duke of Burgundy, who was now the most powerful man in France. On 10 September 1419, however, John the Fearless was murdered while holding discussions with representatives of the Dauphin, an event that prevented any possible reconciliation between the Armagnacs and the Burgundians and finally convinced the latter to throw in their lot with Henry V. Six months later, having no alternative, the mad monarch of France – Charles VI – was forced by the Burgundians to sign the Treaty of Troyes with the English. According to this treaty, Henry V was made regent of France and was officially acknowledged (along with his future sons) as the legitimate successor to the French throne. In practice, Henry was to become King of France upon Charles VI's death. The Treaty of Troyes also arranged for the marriage of Charles VI's daughter to Henry V, which was the first substantial step towards the formation of a dual Anglo-French monarchy. The Dauphin of France, who now guided what remained of the Armagnacs, was completely disinherited. On 2 June 1420, Henry V married Charles VI's daughter, Catherine of Valois, then on 6 December 1421 the couple had a son, named Henry like his father. The signing of the Treaty of Troyes, however, did not bring the Hundred Years' War to an end, since the Dauphin and his Armagnac supporters continued fighting against both the

English longbowman wearing metal helmet and *camail* of mail armour. (*Photo by The Free Company of Aquitaine, copyright by Nic Hawkins*)

English and the Burgundians. The Dauphin established a new military alliance with the Scots, who sent troops to France in order to support the French resistance. In March 1421, an English army of 4,000 soldiers, who had been conducting a raiding expedition inside the territories controlled by the Dauphin was routed by a Franco-Scottish force of 5,000 men at the Battle of Baugé. Following this setback, Henry V decided to return to France to defeat the Dauphin once and for all. While besieging the enemy fortress of Meaux, however, Henry contracted dysentery; a few months later, on 31 August 1422, the King of England died. Henry's infant son was soon crowned King of England as Henry VI, and a few months later also King of France with the name of Henry II following the death of Charles VI.

The English position in France, however, was not a very stable one, as it was heavily dependent upon the support of the Burgundians. Furthermore, the Dauphin was determined to reconquer his kingdom. The Armagnacs never acknowledged Henry VI as their legitimate monarch and continued to fight under the Dauphin's orders in central France. In 1423, English military forces commanded by the Earl of Salisbury defeated Franco-Scottish troops at the Battle of Cravant. Some months later, however, the English suffered a minor setback at the Battle of La Brossinière. English forces in France, under the leadership of the Duke of Bedford, campaigned against Armagnac troops during 1424, with the objective of destroying them in a pitched battle. The French troops numbered around 16,000 men and included 6,000

The full panoply of an English longbowman from the 1410s. (*Photo and copyright by Toxophilus.net*)

English longbowman from the 1410s wearing a skull cap of the Monmouth type made of wool. (*Photo and copyright by Toxophilus.net*)

Scots, as well as 2,000 Italian professional men-at-arms provided by the Duchy of Milan, while the English army comprised around 8,000 men, including a large number of longbowmen. The armies clashed at the Battle of Verneuil on 17 August 1424. Following the Battle of Azincourt, advances and innovations introduced in the production of plate armour had given armoured cavalry a much greater measure of protection against the arrows fired by longbows. This was experienced by the Duke of Bedford at Verneuil, where the defensive positions of his archers were swept away by a frontal charge of the Milanese men-at-arms. Luckily for the duke, however, the English knights stood firm following the successful French attack and – after some bitter fighting – were able to win the day. The Battle of Verneuil was a major setback for the Dauphin, with almost all his Scottish allies being killed, which convinced the Kingdom of Scotland to stop sending troops to the Continent. The period from 1424–28 witnessed the peak of English power in France, with them controlling all the lands from the Channel in the north to the Loire river in the south, and from Brittany in the west to Burgundy in the east. Only a few important strongholds were still controlled by the Dauphin in central France, including the heavily fortified city of Orléans, but even that started to be besieged by Anglo-Burgundian forces in October 1428.

Chapter 5

The Fourth Phase of the War, 1429–1453

By the beginning of 1429, the English had all but isolated Orléans from the rest of the Dauphin's territories by capturing many of the smaller towns that were located around the besieged city on the Loire river. Orléans had an enormous strategic importance for the English, representing the last major obstacle to a general offensive directed against the remainder of the Armagnac territories. When it seemed that the fall of Orléans was imminent, a young French girl named Joan, aged just 17, arrived at the Dauphin's court in Chinon. Joan told the Dauphin that she had come to raise the siege of Orléans and to lead him to Reims for his coronation as King of France; she also said that in a vision she had received precise instructions from God to do so in order to save France from complete destruction. The Dauphin was greatly impressed by the vibrant words of the young girl, mostly because she showed great personal charisma and a strong religious zeal. He and his council, however, needed more assurance before deciding to believe in the words of Joan. They sent her to Poitiers, where she was examined by a council of theologians, who declared that the girl was a sincere person and a good Catholic. The Dauphin, believing that Joan's charisma could inspire his soldiers fighting at Orléans, agreed to send her among his troops. Joan received a full set of plate armour from the Dauphin and designed her own banner, which had on it an image of the Virgin Mary. Joan, who became known as Joan of Arc only after her death, arrived at Orléans on 29 April 1429 and was greeted enthusiastically by the population, her incredible story being already well known. Her strong personality soon began to raise the spirits of the French soldiers, inspiring devotion and the hope of divine assistance. Joan's belief in the divine origin of her mission turned the Anglo-French conflict into a religious war. Initially, Joan was not assigned any formal military command and was not included in military councils, but her popularity grew immensely within days. She was always present when the most intense fighting took place and stayed with the front ranks in order to inspire them with her example. In early May, after having successfully repulsed several enemy attacks, the French went on the offensive and assaulted the fortress of Saint-Loup, which was one of the many fortifications controlled by the English in the area surrounding Orléans. Joan, with her banner in hand, took part in the French assaults and rallied the Armagnac soldiers until they took the fortress. During the

English longbowman from the 1410s wearing a *bascinet* with *camail*. (*Photo and copyright by Toxophilus.net*)

English longbowman from the 1430s wearing an open *sallet*. (*Photo and copyright by Les Lions du Kent*)

English longbowman from the 1430s preparing to shoot his bow.
(*Photo and copyright by Les Lions du Kent*)

following days, one by one, the French recaptured all the fortified positions that were in English hands around Orléans. They took also the main English stronghold, Les Tourelles, after a desperate assault during which Joan was wounded by an arrow between the neck and the shoulder while holding her sacred banner. On 8 May, having suffered a series of defeats, the English abandoned the siege of Orléans.

The great victory, obtained thanks to the decisive role played by Joan, was interpreted by many people as confirming the divine nature of her mission. After her first success, Joan insisted that the French troops should advance promptly towards Reims in order to crown the Dauphin in the city. Before reaching Reims, however, the French needed to recapture all the strategic bridge towns that were located along the course of the Loire river. This new campaign began on 11 June and consisted of a series of minor sieges conducted by the French, with Joan scaling siege ladders with her banner in hand in order to inspire courage and devotion among the assaulting troops. Before the main English army in France could arrive from Paris, the French had already taken all their objectives. On 18 June, the English field forces in central France, around 5,000 men strong, were defeated by a smaller French army at the Battle of Patay. Rather than a large pitched battle, this was essentially a failed English ambush, which cost them significant losses. Following their victory at Patay, the French marched on Reims without meeting further opposition. The city opened its gates on 16 July, and the following morning the Dauphin was crowned as Charles VII. Joan was given a place of honour at the ceremony and announced that God's will had been fulfilled. After a short pause, the French resumed their offensive, aiming to take Paris. Many of the towns encountered along the way surrendered without a fight, and by 8 September they could invest the French capital. The English defences in Paris, however, were too strong for them. Despite their efforts, the French were repulsed with severe losses, and Joan was wounded in the leg by a crossbow bolt. After his troops had been denied by the enemy defences, Charles VII ordered an end to the assault on Paris. After these events, the Armagnacs and the Burgundians initiated a series of peace talks and hostilities were temporarily suspended. While the negotiations were still taking place, however, the Duke of Burgundy started to attack some of the towns that had recently been taken by the Armagnacs. One such town was Compiègne, which was besieged by superior Burgundian forces. Joan, without the permission of Charles VII, set out with a small group of volunteer soldiers at the end of March 1430 in an attempt to relieve Compiègne from the enemy siege. Along the route of their march, Joan's forces were enlarged by the arrival of more volunteers, allowing them to defeat some Anglo-Burgundian troops that they encountered along the way. Joan reached Compiégne on 14 May, and a few days later she launched an attack against the camp of the besieging troops. The attack ended in complete failure, with Joan being captured by the Burgundians. The English, who considered Joan the worst of their French enemies, negotiated with their Burgundian allies to pay Joan's ransom and for her to be transferred to their custody. In November 1430, in exchange for a payment of 10,000 livres tournois, Joan was given to the English. She was then moved to Rouen, where she was put on trial for heresy. Found guilty, she was executed by being burned at the stake on 30 May 1431 at the age of 19.

Despite Joan of Arc's death, by the beginning of the 1430s the fortunes of war had turned dramatically against the English, whose position in France was by now quite weak. Thanks to the decisive role played by Joan, the French had obtained complete control over central France and Charles VII had been able to stabilize his power. The new monarch of France soon showed himself a skilled diplomat and intelligent ruler, working hard to reunify his nation by ending the bitter rivalry that divided the Armagnacs from the Burgundians. At the same time, he also worked to transform his military forces into a modern and centralized army that could expel the English from France once and for all. In the summer of 1435, after the failure of peace negotiations between Charles VII and the Duke of Bedford, the Burgundians decided to terminate their alliance with the English and to make peace with the Armagnacs. As a result, the Duke of Burgundy, Philip the Good, signed the Treaty of Arras with Charles VII. This was of great importance, as it returned Paris to the Armagnacs and officially recognized Charles VII as the only legitimate ruler of France. The end of the long-lasting Anglo-Burgundian alliance was a major blow for the English, who were left without a capable military leader in France after the Duke of Bedford died during 1435. The signing of the Treaty of Arras was followed by a series of long truces, which gave Charles VII time to centralize and modernize his forces. The French monarch transformed his heavy cavalry into a permanent military corps, with superior discipline and training. At the same time, he invested large sums of money in the creation of an impressive artillery train, thanks to which the French could capture enemy strongholds after just a few days of cannon bombardment. By using the same strategy employed by Bertrand du Guesclin several decades before, the French reconquered several areas of northern France with guerrilla tactics and without having to fight a single pitched battle against the English. The English were experiencing serious difficulties in financing the war in France, and Henry VI could not be compared to his father in terms of politico-military vision. By 1444, the English controlled only Normandy and Gascony in France. England was on the verge of bankruptcy, and its French vassals could no longer sustain the heavy taxation that was imposed upon them. As a result, the English agreed to sign the Treaty of Tours with France in order to gain time to improve their defences on the

The Fourth Phase of the War, 1429–1453

Detail of the personal equipment carried by an English longbowman from the 1430s.
(*Photo and copyright by Les Lions du Kent*)

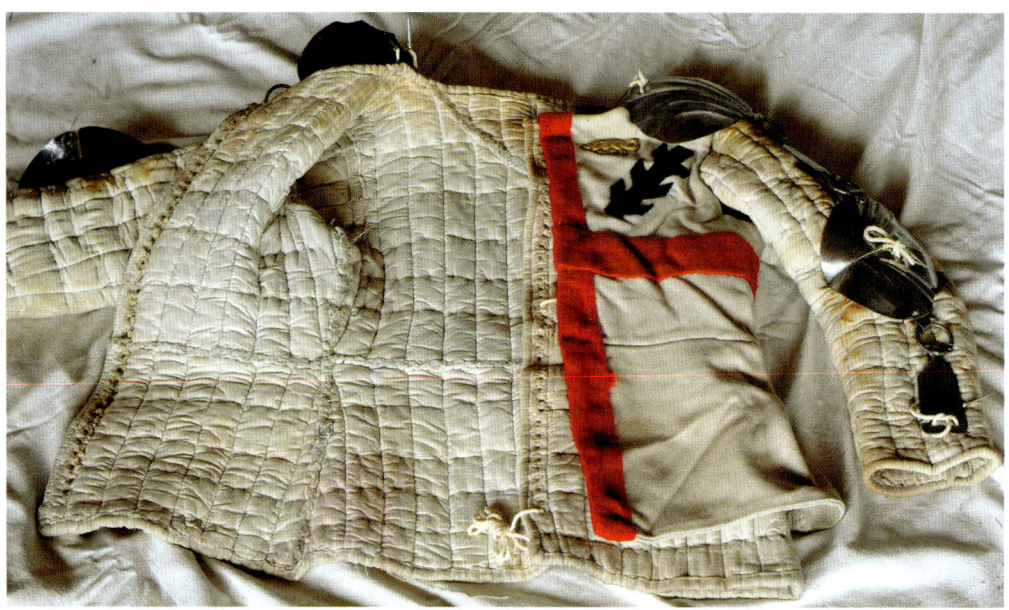

The padded *aketon* of an English longbowman from the 1430s.
(*Photo and copyright by Les Lions du Kent*)

Some elements of an English longbowman's equipment, including a knife and an axe,
as well as a buckler shield. (*Photo and copyright by Les Lions du Kent*)

Continent. When the truce came to an end in 1449, the French prepared for a large-scale invasion of Normandy.

Soon after resuming hostilities in June 1449, the French invested Normandy with their reformed and enlarged army. Many English strongholds located on Norman territory were retaken by Louis VII, mostly thanks to the superiority of his artillery. After a campaign of just a few months, the French had retaken most of Normandy by October, including the important city of Rouen. The English seemed to be unable to respond to these moves, and for several months sent no reinforcements to their garrisons in France. In the winter of 1449, they finally gathered a small army of 3,400 men in Portsmouth and dispatched it to Cherbourg during the following March. The expeditionary force had as its main objective relieving Caen, which had come under French siege during the previous autumn. After obtaining a series of minor victories, the English troops reached Formigny on 14 April 1450, where they were confronted by a French army mustering around 3,000 men. The Battle of Formigny, like several other major encounters of the Hundred Years' War, began with a failed French assault on the English defensive positions. This was followed by an English counter-attack, during which they captured the enemy artillery. When it seemed that the French had been defeated, however, a strong relief force made up of Breton knights reached the battlefield from the south and attacked the English on their left flank. Having abandoned their defensive positions and coming under attack from two directions, the English soldiers were charged upon by the enemy cavalry on the open field and massacred. With no other significant English military contingents remaining in Normandy, Caen was finally captured by the French on 12 June 1450. Some weeks later, on 12 August, the main English stronghold in Normandy – Cherbourg – was also taken by Charles VII. Following the fall of Normandy, the French concentrated their military efforts on Gascony in an attempt to completely liberate their nation. The French conquest of Gascon lands was incredibly rapid, and on 1 November 1450, a numerically inferior Anglo-Gascon force was defeated at the Battle of Blanquefort. Some months later, after a short siege, the Gascon capital of Bordeaux surrendered to Charles VII on 30 June 1451.

After the fall of Bordeaux, it seemed that the Hundred Years' War had come to an end, as the French had occupied the whole of Gascony and the only English holding in France was the port city of Calais. However, the Gascons did not welcome becoming French subjects, fearing – correctly – that the progressive centralization of the French monarchy could damage their economic activities, which was based on trade with England. The most prominent Gascon nobles sent messengers to Henry VI soon after the fall of their territory, demanding that the English monarch assemble an expeditionary force to expel the French from Bordeaux. After some initial hesitation, the king finally decided to raise an army of 3,000 men and despatched it to Gascony. The English troops, commanded by the experienced John Talbot, landed on the Continent on 17 October 1452. Thanks to the effective cooperation of the Gascon population, the English were able to retake Bordeaux quite easily on 23 October. The English invasion, which took the French by surprise, continued with an effective

The full panoply of an English longbowman in Burgundian service from the 1460s.
(*Photo and copyright by Toxophilus.net*)

offensive that led to the reconquest of most of western Gascony by the end of the year. Charles VII had prepared his forces to meet an English invasion, but had been convinced this would materialize in Normandy. During the winter of 1452–53, the French king responded by mobilizing his army so that by early 1453 he was ready to counter-attack in the south. Charles invaded Gascony with three separate armies, all of them aiming for Bordeaux. Talbot, despite his desperate requests for help, received only another 3,000 soldiers from England as reinforcements and thus had to count on the support of the Gascons to counter the enemy invasion. During their advance, the French laid siege to the English stronghold of Castillon, approximately 25 miles east of Bordeaux. Talbot, upon learning that the bulk of the French forces were concentrated around Castillon, set out to relieve the besieged garrison. The garrison's situation was becoming desperate, the French troops besieging Castillon having a large and effective artillery train that consisted of several heavy pieces. These cannons were deployed in a fortified park that consisted of a deep trench with a wall of earth behind it that was strengthened with tree-trunks. The most remarkable feature of the French artillery park was its wavy line of ditches and earthworks, which enabled the guns to enfilade any attackers. In total, the French had around 300 guns of various sizes, which were all manned by expert artillerymen. Upon arriving at Castillon with 500 men-at-arms and 800 mounted archers, Talbot decided to attack the French

English longbowman in Burgundian service from the 1460s, wearing a skull cap of the Monmouth type made of wool. (*Photo and copyright by Toxophilus.net*)

English longbowman in Burgundian service from the 1460s, wearing an open *sallet*. (*Photo and copyright by Toxophilus.net*)

camp in the hope of taking the enemy by surprise. Despite being outnumbered by the French, the English attacked the strong enemy field fortifications with great determination. Nevertheless, the superior firepower of the French guns obliterated the attackers, with each French shot killing at least six English men-at-arms. After the English had already suffered severe losses, the French launched a charge with their elite heavy cavalry against the exposed right flank of the attackers. Badly outnumbered, the English were routed, with Talbot, after fighting with great courage, among those killed. The Battle of Castillon was a disaster for the English cause and a great victory for Charles VII. After Talbot's death, English authority in Gascony eroded quite rapidly. The French retook Bordeaux on 19 October 1453, marking the effective end of the Hundred Years' War.

Soon after the French victory in Gascony, Henry VI lost his mental capacity, leading to the beginning of a new political phase in the history of England. The civil war known as the Wars of the Roses began during 1455, with the forces of the ruling House of Lancaster clashing with the supporters of the rival House of York. The kingdoms of England and France remained formally at war for another two decades after 1453, but the English were in no position to carry on hostilities as their country was ravaged by internecine conflict. The loss of their continental holdings had devastating financial consequences for many of the major English aristocrats, who had invested large sums of money in Gascony for centuries. The formal end of the Hundred Years' War came in 1475, when the Treaty of Picquigny was signed between

Detail of the quiver and leather bag carried by an English longbowman in 1410.
(*Photo and copyright by Toxophilus.net*)

French archer wearing an open *sallet*. (*Photo and copyright by Alliance des Lions d'Anjou*)

French archer equipped with a kettle helmet and leather breastplate.
(*Photo and copyright by La Guerre des Couronnes*)

England and France. By that time, the French monarchy was fighting again against the Duchy of Burgundy in order to annex its lands and wanted to establish positive diplomatic relations with the English. After the events of 1453, the English continued to control the city of Calais in France – which was not seized by the French until 1558 – as well as the Channel Islands, which had always been part of the Duchy of Normandy and are still today part of Great Britain's national territory. The Hundred Years' War was one of the key historical events that led to the transformation of both England and France from medieval feudal monarchies to modern centralized states, with the national feelings that emerged from the long conflict contributing to the definitive unification of both countries. After 1453, the Kingdom of France became Europe's strongest military power and started expanding its territories thanks to the superiority of its army, which was the first permanent and modern military force on the Continent. England, meanwhile, renounced all its expansionist ambitions directed towards mainland Europe, instead focusing all its resources on becoming the world's leading maritime power. The age of the feudal armies made up of knights had come to an end, and new weapons were set to dominate future European battlefields. The era of the longbow and the great mercenary companies was slowly disappearing, opening the way for the ascendancy of large national armies equipped with firearms. From a historical point of view, it is possible to see the long conflict that ran between 1337 and 1453 as a 'bridge' connecting two different eras, representing an age of decisive change for two of Europe's leading nations.

Chapter 6

The Armies of the Hundred Years' War

The English Military Forces

The Norman Conquest that began in 1066 brought feudalism to the Kingdom of England, with King William parcelling out the lands of his new realm to the barons who had fought for him at the Battle of Hastings. According to the latest calculations, around 5,000 knights were enfeoffed – i.e., they were given a fiefdom – by William the Conqueror during the first phase of his reign. The English lands were given not only to lay barons, but also to clerical nobles who were 'Princes of the Church'. Each baron, whether lay or clerical, was required to provide some of the knights who were under his orders to the king in case of war. According to the *Cartae Baronum* of 1166 – a compilation of data detailing the military obligations of all the English nobles – 784 knights out of the 5,000 who could be mobilized by the monarchy were to be provided by clerical barons. Over time, the military system based on sub-infeudation – i.e., the division of the barons' major fiefdoms into minor ones given to knights – became increasingly complex. An important military document from 1181 – the so-called 'Assize of Arms' – prescribed that when the number of knights sub-infeudated within his fiefdom fell short of the knight-service owed to the monarch, a single feudal tenant should maintain sufficient harness to equip some knights from his personal household in order to make up the difference. Most of the English nobles had personal households consisting of loyal knights who provided military service in exchange for money rather than land. These retinues of professional soldiers could consist of just a few individuals but might also be larger contingents, depending on the wealth of the baron paying them. The compulsory military service based on the feudal military structure – known as *servitium debitum* – could last for a maximum of sixty days (later reduced to forty) after mobilization. Initially, the mobilized feudal knights could also be sent to fight overseas, to protect Plantagenet territorial possessions in France, but after the reign of King John, most of the English *milites* (knights) usually refused to serve outside the British Isles.

Some major nobles were granted what was known as 'money fief'; they were not required to send their knights to the king in case of war but had to provide a fixed sum of money with which the monarch could recruit mercenary soldiers. This system, however, never became particularly popular in Plantagenet lands. Feudal military mobilizations usually caused malcontent among the barons of the realm, who were interested in pursuing their own personal interests more than those of the monarchy. As a result, from 1157, the Plantagenet kings attempted to introduce a new form of partial mobilization that was based on a quota system. According to this system, the monarch was to summon only a portion – one third – of those knights owing feudal military service, and to call upon those remaining at home to support the mobilized knights economically through the *scutage* system. The latter was based on a simple principle: if exempted from his military duties, each vassal was to pay a certain sum of money that was to be used for buying and maintaining the personal military equipment of those vassals who had been mobilized. By the end of King John's reign, however, this system of partial mobilization was no longer in use, since it had failed to achieve its objectives. The knights holding a fiefdom, however, were not the only professional soldiers who could be called to serve by a Plantagenet king. There were also tenants of an inferior social status, who were known as 'sergeants'. These, despite not being nobles, had been given a land property by the monarchy in exchange for their military service. Originally, the sergeants were required to serve as heavy infantrymen, since they did not have the economic resources to maintain a horse, but many of them eventually became rich enough to equip themselves exactly like the noble *milites*. It should be noted, however, that the number of sergeants living in the Kingdom of England always remained quite small – especially if compared with their equivalents serving under the King of France.

Cavalry was not the only component of the Plantagenet armies, which also included sizeable contingents of infantrymen. After the Norman Conquest of England, the old *fyrd* military system created by the Saxons a few centuries before was not eradicated. According to this system, each able-bodied free man aged 16–60 and living in any shire of the Kingdom of England could be called to serve by his overlord in case of war. Those individuals who refused military service were subject to fines or the loss of their properties. A commoner, for example, was to pay a fine of 30 shillings if he neglected compulsory military service. Service in the *fyrd* was usually of short duration and had practically no costs for the royal authorities, since the members of this general levy were expected to provide their own arms and provisions and were not paid by the monarch for their military services. Originally, the *fyrd* was mobilized and organized on a local basis, according to the tribal subdivisions of the various communities. However, with the arrival of feudalism, it started to be managed by the feudal lords (thus becoming known as the 'shire *fyrd*'). Each knight could mobilize a certain number of peasants who lived and worked on his land properties in order to form a small retinue of poorly equipped infantrymen. In case of large-scale foreign

French crossbowman wearing a corselet of mail armour. (*Photo and copyright by Alsatiae Protectores*)

French crossbowman wearing a padded *aketon*. (*Photo and copyright by Alliance des Lions d'Anjou*)

invasion, it was the king's responsibility to call up the 'national *fyrd*', which was made up of all the able-bodied men of his realm. Conditions of service for the national *fyrd* (also known as the 'great *fyrd*') and for the more common shire *fyrd* were quite different, since in most cases the English commoners did not welcome the prospect of serving far from their homes for long periods of time. Most of the English freemen were peasants, who spent their lives working in the fields and following natural cycles. As a result, on most occasions, service in the great *fyrd* could last only for very limited periods of time – sixty days, later reduced to forty – and the king had to pay his freemen if any additional period of service was needed. The three most important military documents of the early Plantagenet period – the 1181 'Assize of Arms', the 1242 'Assize' and the 1285 'Statute of Winchester' – all confirmed the existence of the feudal infantry levy.

Since the late Saxon period, a quota system of mobilization existed inside the *fyrd*; on most occasions, in fact, only one freeman from each 5 hides of land was required to join the national *fyrd* when it was mobilized for a campaign. The selected

French crossbowman with a kettle helmet. (*Photo and copyright by Genz d'armes 1415*)

French crossbowman standing near a decorated *pavise* shield.
(*Photo and copyright by Alliance des Lions d'Anjou*)

French crossbowman rearming his weapon. (*Photo and copyright by Alliance des Lions d'Anjou*)

individual was expected to be equipped with spear and shield. In addition, he was expected to have provisions for two months and to receive a wage of 4 shillings that were both provided by the other men living on the 5 hides of land from which he was levied. The Norman kings abolished payments for the members of the *fyrd*, since feudal military service was considered to be a duty for each peasant. During the closing decades of the twelfth century, however, the Plantagenets reintroduced

Detail showing a French crossbow and its darts. (*Photo and copyright by La Guerre des Couronnes*)

them for when the peasant infantrymen were not serving abroad. During the late Saxon period, a new social class of lesser noblemen, the *thegns*, had emerged from the rural communities and had started to hold estates, the average extent of which was 5 hides. After the Norman Conquest, these minor landowners were mostly transformed into sergeants, who were frequently employed by knights as the commanders of their feudal infantry retinues. It should be noted that the smallest contingents of peasant foot soldiers could be commanded by parish priests, while the largest ones were usually led by the local sheriffs. The sheriffs, introduced in England by the Normans, were royal officials responsible for keeping peace in the various shires and for arranging the annual shire payment owed to the king. During the Plantagenet period, the Kingdom of England did not have large urban centres and thus did not see the development of significant urban militias, differently from what happened in France. Only London could mobilize a large number of well-equipped infantrymen (around 6,000) who – differently from their equivalents of the feudal levy – were mostly craftsmen and merchants. The 'Assize of Arms' of 1181, a document promulgated by Henry II and detailing the kind of personal equipment that every knight and feudal infantryman had to carry in war, divided the commoners into three military categories according to their economic capabilities: those possessing at least 16 marks of chattels or rents – like the richest sergeants – were to equip themselves as knights with full panoply; those with at least 10 marks of chattels or rents – like the poorest sergeants – were to equip themselves as heavy infantrymen with helmet, hauberk of mail and spear; and those who had less than 10 marks of chattels or rents were to equip themselves with helmet, quilted *aketon* jacket and spear. Shields, being defensive weapons, were not mentioned in the document, but were carried by all soldiers. Curiously, Henry II also enacted an 'Assize of Arms' for his French territorial domains in 1181, but this prescribed different panoplies for the foot troops belonging to the second and third category. The soldiers of the second category were to have helmet, hauberk of mail, spear and sword; the soldiers of the third category were to have helmet, quilted *aketon*, spear and sword or bow with arrows. These differences are quite interesting, since they show two things: first, that most of the English commoners were too poor to own a sword; second, that the longbow was not yet a popular alternative to the standard infantry spear. Henry III's 'Assize' of 1242 modified the panoply required to each category of freemen. Members of the first category were to have helmet, hauberk of mail, spear, sword and knife; members of the second were to have helmet, quilted *aketon*, spear, sword and knife; and members of the third could have bow, sword and knife or a single 'peasant weapon' (such as a falchion – a single-edged sword – or gisarme battle axe). The most important innovation was the introduction of the bow as an alternative to the standard infantry weapons used by the third category.

Under Edward I, the nature of England's military forces changed considerably. First of all, knights and peasant infantrymen recruited according to the feudal system rapidly became a secondary component of the English army. They were replaced by professional soldiers who served for money and without limitations of time/space (which had always hampered the expansionist campaigns of the previous Plantagenet kings). The personal household of the monarch, known as the *familia regis*, had previously consisted of just a few knights acting as the personal bodyguard of the king; under Edward I, it was greatly expanded and came to comprise a few hundreds of knights and mounted sergeants who served for money and responded only to the monarch. These were usually organized into 'constabularies' that had an average strength of 100 *milites stipendiarii* ('paid knights') each. The feudal knights, instead, served in small groups of between five and fifteen, which were the direct heirs of the *conrois* units employed in the Norman armies. A variable number of *conrois* could be assembled together to form the larger *batailles*, or 'battles' – the cavalry divisions deployed for pitched battles. Each knight, whether feudal or mercenary, was usually accompanied on the battlefield by one or two esquires. These played only an auxiliary role and were tasked with managing the three horses owned by each knight – the *destrier* or war horse, the *courser* employed for travelling long distances and the *rouncey* used for transporting equipment. However, the esquires could also fight as light cavalrymen in case of emergency. The royal household, in addition to the *milites stipendiarii*, started to include increasing numbers of foreign mercenaries recruited from abroad (mostly from the remaining Plantagenet French possessions in Gascony). The great majority of the Gascon mercenaries were mounted crossbowmen, who moved on horse but fought on foot. The crossbow never became popular in England, due to the ascendancy of the longbow as a national weapon, so the crossbowmen of the English Plantagenet armies were all foreign mercenaries. Edward I, during his conquest of Wales, understood that the local longbowmen had enormous combat potential and soon started to recruit large numbers of them for his military forces. Around 1285, almost two-thirds of the infantrymen serving in the English army were Welsh longbowmen, who had replaced the previous feudal infantry levies. Edward I also sponsored the adoption of the longbow as the standard weapon of the English commoners, since he did not want to rely in future entirely on Welsh archers. These Welsh archers were usually organized on constabularies with 100 men each, like their English equivalents. The previous contingents of feudal infantry were usually organized on larger constabularies with 500 men each, but these had mostly disappeared by the beginning of Edward I's reign. A single constabulary of 100 infantrymen was usually divided into five sub-units, with twenty soldiers each. Each constabulary was commanded by an officer – equipped as a mounted sergeant – who was known as a *centenar*, while each sub-unit was under the orders of a sort of NCO – equipped as a foot sergeant – called a *vintenar*.

The 1285 'Statute of Winchester', which remained valid until the beginning of the Hundred Years' War, modified in a sensible way the panoply that each category of English soldiers had to carry on the battlefield. It divided the English subjects who could be called to serve into six distinct categories, always formulated according to the economic capabilities of their members. The first category included individuals who owned more than £40 of land, who were required to equip themselves as heavy knights. The second category included those who owned more than £20 of land, who were to equip themselves as mounted sergeants. The third category included individuals who owned more than £15 of land, who had to equip themselves as heavy infantrymen with mail hauberk. The fourth category was for men who owned more than £10 of land, who were required to equip themselves as medium infantrymen with quilted *aketon*. The fifth category included those who owned more than £2 of land, who were to equip themselves as longbowmen (with bow, sword and knife). The final category included men who owned less than £2 of land, who could arm themselves

French crossbow. (*Photo and copyright by Genz d'armes 1415*)

with a longbow or whatever 'peasant weapon' they might have. With the promulgation of the 'Statute of Winchester', the standard procedures for mobilization were also changed. In case of war, the king was to appoint a Commission of Array, made up of experienced knights, usually coming from the royal household. These were tasked with recruiting the necessary number of soldiers from the various shires and urban centres of the realm and then assembling them into constabularies. Military service was performed at the individual's expense if conducted within the boundaries of his country, but at the king's expense if outside those boundaries.

During the early fourteenth century, the Plantagenet monarchs started recruiting military contingents in a new way, according to the 'indenture system'. This worked quite simply: the king stipulated a formal contract with one of his nobles for raising a certain number of soldiers for a precise period of time, in exchange for the payment of a predetermined sum of money. The name of the new system derived from the

Man-at-arms preparing himself for battle; the plate armour has not yet been placed over the mail. (*Photo and copyright by Alliance des Lions d'Anjou*)

Man-at-arms preparing himself for battle; the padded *aketon* is partly visible under his mail. (*Photo and copyright by Alliance des Lions d'Anjou*)

fact that each contract had an indented edge that, in order to prevent forgery, had to match perfectly with the corresponding indents placed on the top or bottom edge of its counterfoil, which was stored in the royal archives. The creation of the indenture system was the result of the feudal military organization's gradual collapse. During the early Plantagenet period, the English barons were obliged to send their knights to the king in case of war, while by the beginning of the fourteenth century, the monarch had to pay his nobles in exchange for their military services, exactly if they were mercenary warlords. During the whole Plantagenet period, the English military forces were always supplemented by sizeable contingents of mercenaries recruited from abroad. Since the English knights and feudal levies were always reluctant to serve overseas, the Plantagenet armies fighting in France mostly consisted of two categories of troops: local knights/feudal levies from the French regions that were under Plantagenet control, and mercenaries from various areas of France or from more distant regions (like Wales or Flanders). After a portion of Ireland was occupied by the English, Plantagenet armies also started to include some contingents of Irish auxiliaries. These consisted of feudal levies that were made up of light infantrymen, who were recruited by the Anglo-Irish lords who owned fiefdoms in the newly conquered areas of Ireland. Initially, the feudal contingents recruited by the Plantagenets in their French territorial possessions were of excellent quality and quite large, especially those from Normandy. These troops, however, could not be employed outside their home territories and usually refused to serve for long periods of time. They were organized and equipped very similarly to their English equivalents. However, the French infantrymen in Plantagenet service included sizeable numbers of well-armed urban militiamen as well as well-trained crossbowmen. After most of the Plantagenet domains in France were lost during King John's reign, only Gascony remained under permanent English control. The military forces of the latter region included feudal contingents raised by the most prominent local nobles as well as urban militiamen from major Gascon cities such as Bordeaux.

In 1346, Edward III revised the Statute of Winchester by introducing nine different categories of troop types. The first included individuals who owned more than £100 of land, who were required to provide four men-at-arms. The second category comprised individuals who owned more than £50 of land, who were to provide two men-at-arms. The third category included those who owned more than £40 of land, who had to provide one man-at-arms as well as one 'hobilar' light cavalryman and one mounted archer. The fourth category consisted of individuals who owned more than £30 of land, who were required to provide one man-at-arms and one mounted archer. The fifth category were men who owned more than £25 of land, who were to provide one man-at-arms. The sixth category included individuals who owned more

Man-at-arms preparing himself for battle; he is already wearing the *fauld* made up of several metal scales. (*Photo and copyright by Alliance des Lions d'Anjou*)

French aristocrat wearing his rich civilian clothes. (*Photo and copyright by Les Lions du Kent*)

French herald bearing the banner of his feudal lord. (*Photo and copyright by La Guerre des Couronnes*)

than £20 of land, who had to provide two hobilar light cavalrymen. The seventh category comprised those who owned more than £10 of land, who were obliged to provide one hobilar light cavalryman. The eighth category included individuals who owned more than £5 of land, who were to provide one mounted archer. Members of the final category, who owned more than £2 of land, were required to provide one foot archer. As is clear from the above, Edward III introduced two new elements in the English military structure: the hobilar light cavalryman and the mounted archer. The term 'hobildar' probably derived from the Norman word 'hobby', which was used to designate the small horses used by the mounted troops of Britain's Celtic nations (Scotland and Ireland). The hobildars were an updated version of the light cavalry provided by the feudal squires: they were mounted on horses of mediocre quality and were tasked with supporting the heavy knights by performing a series of auxiliary duties.

Mounted archers did not belong to the cavalry, being normal archers who owned a horse and used it to travel long distances. Being mounted infantrymen, they had a high degree of mobility and soon became a fundamental component of the English military forces. Mounted archers became so popular during the reign of Edward III that he decided in 1356 to form a Royal Bodyguard consisting of 120 mounted archers. These were recruited from Cheshire and continued to exist as a permanent military corps – paid directly by the king – over the following decades. Their number was later increased to 300–400, and the Black Prince also started to have a personal guard of 100 Cheshire mounted archers. On the battlefield, all English archers usually deployed in strong defensive formations, which were protected by rough-cut stakes. Albeit very simple, these stakes proved extremely effective against the charges of the French heavy cavalry. Thanks to the working tools that they always carried with them, the English archers were capable of building field defences and acting as combat engineers when needed. During battles, they operated in conjunction with the dismounted knights and the infantrymen equipped with polearms, the latter of whom were deployed behind the longbowmen when the army was defending but marched ahead of them when the army was attacking. Following Edward III's death in 1377, the system of feudal recruitment described above was all but abandoned, being replaced quite rapidly by the indenture system. This new system was initially created to provide permanent garrisons to key fortifications, but was later modified in order to recruit the large military contingents that were needed to campaign in France. If an indentured man wished to extend his length of service, he was allowed to do so, thanks to special clauses that were included in most of the contracts. Some indentures were even for life and were valid also in time of peace. Payment could be in the form of fiefs and pensions, but most of the indentured soldiers preferred being

The Armies of the Hundred Years' War   151

Infantryman wearing his civilian clothes, including a soft cap. (*Photo and copyright by Genz d'ordennance*)

Infantryman wearing his civilian clothes, including a wicker hat. (*Photo and copyright by Genz d'armes 1415*)

Infantryman cutting wood in a forest. (*Photo and copyright by Genz d'ordennance*)

paid with money (usually a quarter-year in advance). If their pay fell more than a half-year in arrears, then the contract was deemed annulled. An indentured captain raised the forces his indenture required by sub-contracting, though the nucleus of his troops usually tended to be provided by his own permanent retainers if he was a feudal noble. The indentured soldiers usually included three distinct categories of cavalrymen – 'bannerets' (or officers), men-at-arms and hobildars – plus English archers and Gascon light infantrymen known as bidowers, who were paid like a longbowman but were equipped with throwing javelins and a buckler. Over time, the number of noble knights among the men-at-arms declined considerably due to the great changes that took place in the English social structures. At the same time, foot archers were almost completely replaced by mounted archers, so that by the beginning of the fifteenth century the basic tactical unit of the English army consisted of the following elements: one man-at-arms, one page (paid by the man-at-arms) and three mounted archers. The latter were accompanied on campaign by bowyers, stringers and fletchers in order to keep their bows in good repair and to maintain an adequate supply of bowstrings and arrows. The governing of indentured companies, which typically consisted of 500 men, was covered by the ordinances of war issued at various times during the Hundred Years' War. These official documents specified that no man could stay in the army unless his captain and his company were part of it, nor could he depart on some foray on his own. All companies were required to muster whenever called upon to do so, and it was forbidden for captains to entice men from other companies in order to fill gaps in their own unit.

The English armies fighting in France during the Hundred Years' War comprised significant contingents of Welsh soldiers, who were equipped as archers in most cases as the deadly longbow was the primary weapon of the Welsh commoners. The Welsh contingents, however, also included sizeable numbers of spearmen. The Welsh troops were summoned by royal commissions of array, similarly to what happened with the English feudal contingents. Their recruitment was issued to the Marcher Lords, the English aristocrats who controlled the strategically important border areas located between Wales and England (where several impressive castles had been built during the previous decades). The Welsh units were organized similarly to the English ones, consisting of companies that mustered around 100 fighters each. Curiously, each such unit included an interpreter known as a 'latinier', who was tasked with translating orders from English to Welsh because until the end of the fourteenth century most of the Welsh soldiers continued to speak only their native language. By the outbreak of the Hundred Years' War, the English had not yet completed the conquest of Ireland, but already controlled significant portions of the island, where an Anglo-Irish aristocracy had long since emerged. The Irish contingents serving in France mostly consisted of infantry spearmen recruited by the Anglo-Irish lords according to the usual feudal system, but there were also some small numbers of men-at-arms and hobilars provided by the Anglo-Irish nobility.

Gascony was the only part of England's French possessions that remained in English hands throughout the Hundred Years' War, and as such it provided a significant contribution to the English war efforts. The rich French region of Aquitaine, including Gascony, came into English possession as far back as 1152. Consequently, by the early fourteenth century, its inhabitants no longer thought of themselves as French and were extremely loyal towards the English Crown. During the Hundred Years' War, the Gascon aristocrats and their feudal retinues fought on several occasions in defence of their home territories, and were often also contracted and paid in exactly the same way as English troops to campaign outside the boundaries of Gascony. The Gascon men-at-arms were well known for their

The full panoply of a standard man-at-arms. (*Photo and copyright by Les Lions du Kent*)

The full panoply of a standard heavy infantryman. (*Photo and copyright by Les Lions du Kent*)

courage in battle and their excellent heavy equipment, which was of the same quality as that employed by their French opponents. The Gascon feudal levies, however, consisted almost entirely of lightly equipped infantrymen, either bidowers or brigans. The bidowers, as mentioned above, were skirmishers equipped with a small shield and throwing javelins, while the brigans were irregulars who performed only auxiliary duties and equipped themselves with whatever improvised peasant weapons were available. Regarding the non-Gascon territories that the English controlled during the course of the Hundred Years' War, it should be pointed out that garrisons were retained in captured French fortresses – largely by using the indenture system – from the very beginning of the conflict. At the same time, fiefs were granted in occupied territory exactly like happened on English soil.

Up to the beginning of the fifteenth century, the instrument of English military success in France was the expeditionary force, which was recruited by contract according to the system already described and usually served for short periods of time. A standard expeditionary force cost much less than military occupation and was relatively easy to control. However, from the 1380s, it became apparent that a more stable English military presence was needed on French soil because the English

Detail of a *camail* made of metal scales. (*Photo and copyright by La Guerre des Couronnes*)

conquests on the Continent were in the process of being consolidated as permanent settlements. As a result, indentures started to be drawn up annually in order to provide permanent garrisons to the most important fortifications and urban centres of the English domains in France. Individually, the English military garrisons on the Continent were not particularly large, but cumulatively they constituted a sizeable military presence. They were supported by the indentured retinues of the various

Detail of a *bascinet* helmet. (*Photo and copyright by Alliance des Lions d'Anjou*)

nobles who had been assigned fiefdoms in France and constituted the first line of defence in case of French attack. By the time the English territorial possessions in France reached their greatest extent, there were around 8,000 soldiers serving on a permanent basis on the Continent and performing garrison duties. The English, in

Detail of a *sallet* helmet worn open. (*Photo and copyright by La Guerre des Couronnes*)

some cases, could also count on the contingents of urban militia recruited by the communal governments of the French cities that were under their control; these, which often included many crossbowmen, were called '*Faux Français*', or 'False French', by their enemies.

Back view of a corselet made of hardened leather. (*Photo and copyright by Alliance des Lions d'Anjou*)

Regarding the development of artillery, the English were probably the first in Europe to employ field pieces during a major pitched battle. At the Battle of Crécy, they fired upon the Genoese crossbowmen in French service with several guns. English artillery pieces were initially produced only in the Tower of London, but from the 1370s new manufacturing centres appeared. By the beginning of the fifteenth century, most of the major English cities had guns, and field pieces customarily accompanied all

English armies campaigning on the Continent. It should be noted, however, that the English guns were much smaller and less numerous compared with those deployed by the French during the final phase of the Hundred Years' War.

The French Military Forces

In France, the feudal military system emerged during the turbulent years of the ninth century, which saw the collapse of the Carolingian Empire and the almost complete disappearance of any form of central government. Dependence on the nobility for military support greatly weakened the various monarchs who ruled France until the ascendancy of Philip Augustus. During the course of the tenth century, the six most powerful nobles of the country – the Duke of Normandy, Duke of Burgundy, Duke of France (controlling the region known as Ile de France, centred on Paris), Duke of Aquitaine, Count of Toulouse and Count of Flanders – stripped the French crown practically bare of military power. They transformed the military obligations of their vassals so that service previously owed directly to the king was now owed to them personally. By 987, as a result of this process, the royal demesne had dwindled to a single city and its environs. The new Capetian dynasty founded in 987 did not change the existing situation in any significant way, as during the following two centuries the French monarchs continued to be totally dependent on their aristocrats to raise armies. The French nobles spent most of their energies in opposing the monarchy rather than supporting it. In addition, they were divided by long-lasting rivalries that frequently escalated into feudal wars that were fought on a local basis. The Capetian kings, luckily for the French monarchy, were also dukes of France, and as such could count on the feudal military forces levied from the Paris area. Like their English equivalents, the French monarchs had ecclesiastical feudal lords among their vassals. These, in most cases, were more loyal than the lay nobles. Feudal military service, at least formally, was owed for a standard forty-day period, but it could be extended in exchange for pay if the vassal wished to remain. Service was not obligatory outside the territory of the Kingdom of France, even for pay; some of the major vassals argued that it was not even due outside their own territorial possessions. The feudal magnates supplied only token contingents to the royal government, which were usually very small. By 1180, at the time of the ascendancy of Philip Augustus to the throne, the French crown could count on just 436 knights provided by the various vassals. In case of national emergency, the king could summon a form of general mobilization known as the '*arrière-ban*' that obliged all able-bodied free men aged 18–60 to perform military service. Such a mobilization, however, usually failed to meet the expectations of the royal government, since the various local contingents had to be organized by the major vassals of the realm. Philip Augustus strove to change the existing military situation, particularly by expanding the lands that were part of the royal demesne. Following the Battle of Bouvines in 1214, he deprived some of his major vassals of key regions and annexed vast areas – including Normandy – that had previously been under English control. Thanks to the financial resources emanating from the new territories of the royal demesne, Philip Augustus started recruiting increasingly large contingents of mercenaries, which were placed under the direct control of the king and were paid through the introduction of the *scutage* tax within the royal demesne. By paying the new tax, a royal vassal could avoid compulsory military service. The royal mercenaries eventually consisted of 260 knights, 270 mounted sergeants, eighty-five mounted crossbowmen, 135 foot crossbowmen, 2,000 foot sergeants and 300 *routiers* pikemen. Mounted sergeants and foot sergeants were much more common in the Kingdom of France than in England. These were minor land tenants who earned a living by serving as professional soldiers and could equip themselves with good quality weapons. The *routiers* were heavy infantrymen recruited from Brabant, equipped with long pikes and trained to deal with heavy cavalry charges. They were the only 'foreign' mercenaries in French service. Most of the Crown's mercenaries were employed as garrison troops in time of peace, and were fully mobilized only in time of war in order to form the backbone of the French armies.

Under Philip Augustus, the *scutage* tax became a fundamental feature of French feudalism, as obligatory military service started to be a serious bone of contention between the monarch and his vassals. By 1274, the commutation or fine required in place of service was standardized and the French kings could thus start hiring increasingly large numbers of mercenaries with the money derived from the *scutage* tax. By the beginning of the reign of Philip Augustus, the old feudal militia raised in the various parishes of the kingdom from commoners was no longer in existence and thus could not be mobilized. However, the various urban centres of France had started to organize themselves as communes with their own local laws and military contingents. Philip Augustus granted royal charters to many French cities, not least because he valued highly the militia contingents that they were able to raise. Such troops were perfect for performing garrison duties in frontier areas, but could also provide reliable contingents of infantry for major campaigns. By the time of the Battle of Bouvines, the thirty major communes of France could field a total of 5,140 foot sergeants. During the following decades, their military capabilities increased significantly and the foot sergeants started to be supplemented by sizeable numbers of crossbowmen. The urban militias could be called upon for a period of three months a year, although service could be avoided by paying a sum of money, similarly to what happened with the feudal contingents. The militiamen, from the closing decades of the thirteenth century, equipped themselves in different ways according to their personal financial capabilities. Individuals possessing a revenue of 60 livres or more had to carry a hauberk, helmet, sword and knife; those with a revenue of 30 livres or more were to carry an *aketon*, sword and knife; anyone with a revenue of 10 livres or more had to carry a helmet, sword and knife; and those possessing a revenue of less than 10 livres carried a bow and knife. By the beginning of the fourteenth century, as is made clear from the above, military service in France began to be based largely on the value of possessions, exactly as already happened in England. Each French noble had to provide one fully equipped knight for every 500 livres of his personal revenue, while the lower social classes had to supply six sergeants for every 100 subjects. Military service started to be due from all freemen aged over 18, for a period of four months per year.

At the beginning of the Hundred Years' War, the French armies still had the general structure described in the previous paragraphs and feudal summons remained one of the principal means of recruitment. The feudal military forces of France, however, experienced a long period of decay following the end of Philip Augustus's long reign. Feudal troops started to be paid exactly like the mercenaries and sub-infeudation was largely replaced by the granting of money-fiefs or the stipulation of non-feudal contracts – called 'alliances' – that were quite similar to the English indentures. During the fourteenth century, the general mobilization of the *arrière-ban* began to be applied only to the nobles and not all the able-bodied French subjects. Aristocrats could also avoid mobilization by paying a special tax, but this did not happen very frequently because fighting for the king was crucial to a French noble's status. By 1337, the French heavy cavalry made up of feudal nobles was still considered to be the most effective fighting force in Europe, due to its prestige that derived from archaic notions of chivalrous warfare. Although chivalry was largely out of date by the beginning of the fourteenth century, it remained an important component of the contemporary military ideology. The disastrous Battle of Crécy showed the rest of Europe that the elite French men-at-arms, despite their excellent equipment and training, were no longer invincible. The English longbowmen were more than a match for them, so the French military urgently needed reforming. In 1351, the royal government promulgated a very detailed military ordinance, which tried to innovate as much as possible the organization of the French troops. It concentrated on pay, equipment and administration of the heavy cavalry, one of its main objectives being eliminating the large number of knights who served independently from the contingents commanded by the major nobles. The presence of such independent fighters caused significant organizational and disciplinary problems.

The royal ordinance of 1351 divided the members of the French fighting forces into seven distinct categories, each of which received a different pay: knight '*banneret*'

The Armies of the Hundred Years' War

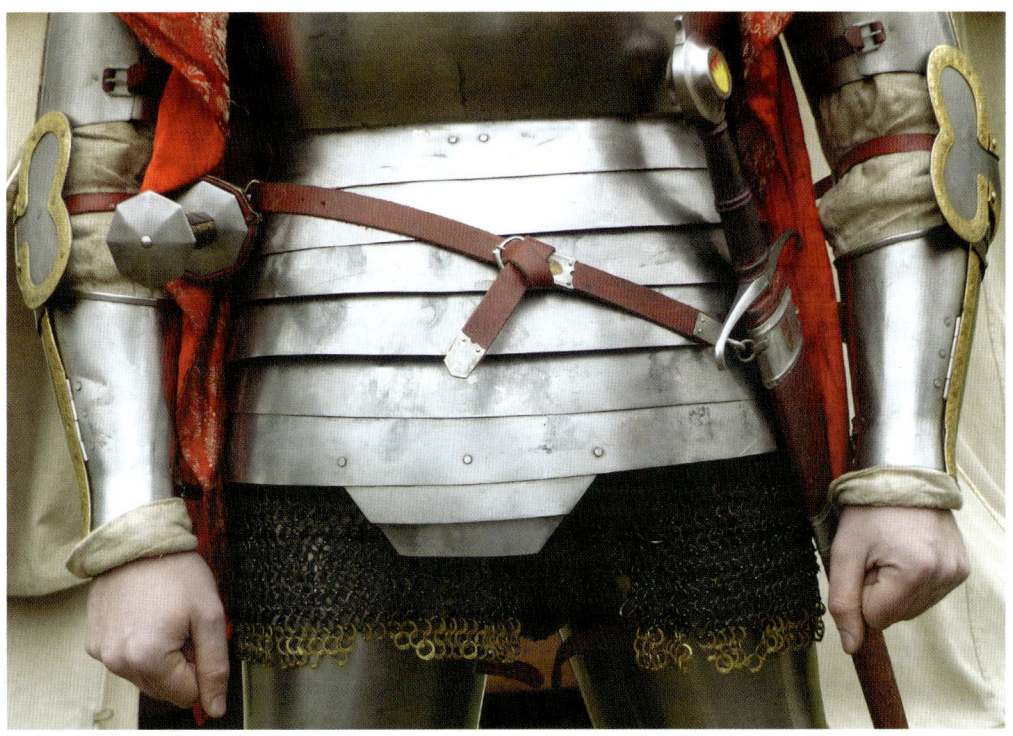

Detail of an armour's *fauld*. (*Photo and copyright by Genz d'armes 1415*)

Detail of an armour's *pauldrons*. (*Photo and copyright by Genz d'armes 1415*)

Detail of an armour's *vambrace*. (*Photo and copyright by La Guerre des Couronnes*)

or officer, knight, squire, valet or mounted infantryman (more or less the equivalent of the English hobildar), crossbowman, *pavisier* (infantryman equipped with *pavise* shield) and armour-bearer (a sort of auxiliary worker). Each man was recorded by name on a muster roll together with a list of his personal equipment and a description of his horse, if he had one (horses were branded for identification). Musters were taken at least twice a month and inspections were conducted on a regular basis, with discipline preserved thanks to the introduction of a punitive system based on fines. From an organizational point of view, the ordinance ordered that all men-at-arms had to be brought together into companies, which ranged in size from a minimum of twenty-five to a maximum of eighty knights, according to the prestige and means of their noble commanders. Transfer from one company to another was forbidden and each officer was responsible for the training of his company. The infantry was organized on small companies, each having between twenty-five and thirty men and commanded by an officer known as a constable, who received double-pay. The men-at-arms and infantrymen who did not have a leader and served singularly were assembled together into companies, with a captain who was appointed by the royal government. While the royal ordinance of 1351 was innovative from a formal point of view, when applied on the field it failed to reach its objectives due to the widespread corruption that afflicted the French military apparatus. As a result, the French suffered another major setback at the Battle of Poitiers. In 1357, there was the first attempt to establish a standing field army, when new taxes were introduced in order to maintain a contingent of 3,000 professional men-at-arms who were to serve on a permanent basis. This new body of knights was supported by a standing corps of crossbowmen, known as the *Corporation des Arbaletiers de Paris*, which by 1373 consisted of 800 professional crossbowmen. Based in Paris, this unit received pay and rations at the expense of the urban government. Similar corporations existed in other major cities of France, but differently from that of Paris they never served outside the territory of their home commune. Paris, in addition to the elite Corporation of Crossbowmen, also fielded a large urban militia of some 6,000–7,000 infantrymen.

In 1374, the royal government implemented a new ordinance which stipulated that all men-at-arms should be grouped into companies of 100 men each. If a company had less than 100 knights, it was to join another unit and could not have its own independent commander. Musters were now called for on a monthly basis, with a tighter control on fraud made possible by a general revision of the method used to pay troops. Before 1374, the captains received pay for their entire companies, but following the introduction of the new system they were paid only for their personal services and their companies were divided into smaller administrative units called *chambres*. Each of the latter mustered ten men and had a leader, who received his pay and that

Detail of an armour's rounded *couter* (elbow armour). (*Photo and copyright by La Guerre des Couronnes*)

of the other nine men of the *chambre*. As we have seen, during most of the Hundred Years' War, the forces of France continued to be made up of feudal contingents raised by the many nobles of the country. Despite their excellent reputation, the French heavy cavalry were defeated on several occasions by the much more reliable English archers. Consequently, during the last years of the Hundred Years' War, the French monarchs started to reform their military forces by adopting drastic measures. Their main objectives were two-fold: modernizing the heavy cavalry and submitting it to the royal authority, and creating a professional body of infantrymen with the same standards of service as the English foot troops.

In 1445, the best elements of the existing noble cavalry were assembled together in order to form a permanent new military corps: the *Compagnies d'Ordonnance*. This consisted of fifteen cavalry companies, the last of which was to act as a mounted bodyguard of the king. Each company was structured on 100 units called 'Spears', each comprising six fighters: one man-at-arms, one squire (known as a *coutilier*), one servant and three mounted archers. The presence of the archers was the result of the great impression caused by the English bowmen on French battlefields during the previous decades. The *Compagnies d'Ordonnance* initially deployed 9,000 mounted fighters. Around 1498, a fourth archer was added to each Spear; later, under Francis I,

Detail of an armour's pointed *couter*. (*Photo and copyright by Alliance des Lions d'Anjou*)

Detail of an armour's gauntlet. (*Photo and copyright by La Guerre des Couronnes*)

a fifth archer was added and the light cavalryman *coutilier* was replaced by a second servant. The *Compagnies d'Ordonnance* also had to be ready to serve in time of peace, and were regularly inspected by royal officers who controlled the quality of their equipment and horses. Thanks to the creation of this new permanent cavalry corps, the French king could avoid using the unreliable feudal contingents. Due to the success of the *Compagnies d'Ordonnance*, something similar was created to replace the feudal infantry that performed garrison duties in the many fortresses around France. This new corps, the *Mortes-payes*, consisted of 900 dismounted Spears with four members each (one man-at-arms, two archers and one servant). The reform of the French infantry, however, proved to be much more difficult than that of the cavalry. In 1448, an important royal order was issued by King Charles VII, according to which in each parish of the Kingdom of France an archer was chosen from among the most apt in the use of weapons. The chosen man was known as a *Franc-archer* and was exempt from direct taxation, in exchange for which and other privileges he had to practice shooting with the bow every Sunday and hold himself ready to march with full equipment in case of royal mobilization. It is possible to see the new semi-permanent militia of the *Franc-archers* as the first French attempt to have some professional infantry. However, these new troops soon showed their deficiencies on the battlefield: they lacked training and keeping them in good order cost a lot of money to the central administration of the state. As a result, in 1481, the *Franc-archers* were temporarily disbanded. They were re-raised during 1485, but only to be employed as a local militia with purely defensive tasks. The corps was definitively disbanded in 1535. From an organizational point of view, the *Franc-archers* were initially grouped into companies of 200–300 men, and later into 'ensigns' with 500 archers each.

In addition to the reform of the cavalry, 1445 also saw the official creation of the French Royal Guard when the first Company of Bodyguards was formed by assembling together 300 Scottish soldiers. Charles VII wanted to have a Royal Guard made up of reliable men, whose loyalty could not be influenced by any external factor, the only way to achieve this being to recruit the new guardsmen from the best foreign soldiers in French service. The Scots were an obvious choice, since they had served for decades as allies of the French in the Hundred Years' War. The new unit was commonly known as the Scottish Guard and initially consisted of 100 heavily armed knights plus 200 foot archers, all its members coming from the lesser nobility of Scotland. The French nobles were completely excluded from service in the Royal Guard, since most of them were prone to revolt against the king and could thus represent a potential threat to him. The 300 members of the Scottish Guard were later divided into two companies: the 100 heavy knights were known as the *Gentilshommes à bec-de-corbin* ('Gentlemen with ravens' beaks') due to the pointed shape of their war hammers, while the 200 archers of the second company became known as the Small Bodyguard because they served on foot. In 1474, it was decided to open the ranks of the Royal Guard to French nobles, and this led to the creation of another two companies. All the new French recruits were veterans, since one of the requirements needed to enter the Royal Guard was to have served for at least three years in the army. By the beginning of the sixteenth century, only the first of the four Guard companies (each of which was 100 strong) was still made up of Scottish soldiers. During the Hundred Years' War, the French deployed sizeable contingents of foreign soldiers, which mostly came from Scotland and the Italian city of Genoa (located not far from the Mediterranean coastline of France). The Scots – who along with France were the fiercest enemies of England during most of the Middle Ages – became a significant component of the French military after 1415, providing sizeable contingents of men-at-arms and archers that participated in several major engagements. The Scottish soldiers fighting on the Continent were not mercenaries but allies, since their kingdom had undertaken several treaties of alliance with France.

Detail of an armour's painted gauntlet. (*Photo and copyright by La Guerre des Couronnes*)

The Genoese soldiers in French service, however, were true mercenaries. For most of the Middle Ages, the city of Genoa was one of the most prominent naval powers of the Mediterranean. The Genoese, in particular, became famous for the excellent quality of their naval infantry, which comprised sizeable numbers of crossbowmen. Over time, increasing numbers of these started to be hired for duty on land by the French, who hoped to counter the firepower of the English archers with that of the Genoese crossbowmen. Genoa was traditionally divided into eight neighbourhoods, known as *compagne*, which were assembled into four couples in order to provide

Detail of an armour's *cuisse* and greave. (*Photo and copyright by La Guerre des Couronnes*).

Detail of an armour's *poleyn*. (*Photo and copyright by La Guerre des Couronnes*)

military contingents. The Genoese military structure included three categories of troops: an active militia formed by professional soldiers paid by the Genoese Republic (mostly crossbowmen, but also knights), a reserve militia consisting of all the able-bodied citizens (mobilized in the *compagne*) and the mercenary troops recruited outside the Republic in case of military emergency. Consequently, Genoa could always count on a central military force made up of professional soldiers: these were mostly crossbowmen (*balistari*), serving on the warships of the Genoese fleet and organized into companies of twenty men each (*bandiere*) that were commanded by a *connestabile*. Each professional soldier was paid and treated as a mercenary by the Genoese Republic, even if he came from the city of Genoa, with periods of service varying from three to six months. Professional crossbowmen were recruited by two noble officials, who received this task from the communal authorities. If one of the chosen crossbowmen proved unable to perform military service, the officer who had recruited him was obliged to reimburse the state with his own money. The standard militia, similar in all aspects to the military forces of the other Italian *comuni*, was to be mobilized only in case of large-scale conflict. At the Battle of Crécy, the French deployed a total of 6,000 Genoese mercenary crossbowmen, who were completely defeated by the English longbowmen. This badly affected the military reputation of the Italian mercenaries, who were recruited in smaller numbers during the second half of the fourteenth century.

Regarding the development of artillery, the most important cities of France already had sizeable numbers of guns by the 1360s. By the beginning of the fifteenth century, most of the leading French aristocrats had purchased artillery pieces for their personal forces. However, the royal government had little artillery of its own, normally having to obtain pieces for a specific campaign by borrowing them from the major cities. From the beginning of their use on the battlefield, French guns were heavier than those of the English, but they started to be employed in an effective way only after Jean Bureau was nominated Master of the Artillery in 1434. The French artillery, once reformed by Bureau, played a key role during the many sieges that took place in the last phase of the Hundred Years' War. By 1458, the French Master of the Artillery commanded a small permanent corps made up of thirty gunners, who operated around forty pieces. By the 1460s, the French artillery train was considered to be the most formidable in Europe.

Equipment

At the beginning of the Plantagenet period, the English and French *milites* were still mainly protected by a hauberk, or shirt of mail, which was made of several thousand

Detail of an armour's *cuisses* and *poleyns*. (*Photo and copyright by La Guerre des Couronnes*)

interlocking metal rings. The dimensions of each hauberk could vary considerably, since the sleeves could reach only to the elbow or be full arm-length. A hauberk generally reached down to the knees, but could be longer or shorter. Producing this kind of armour was a long and costly process, which only nobles could sustain, but the use of mail among knights was practically universal. By the middle of the twelfth

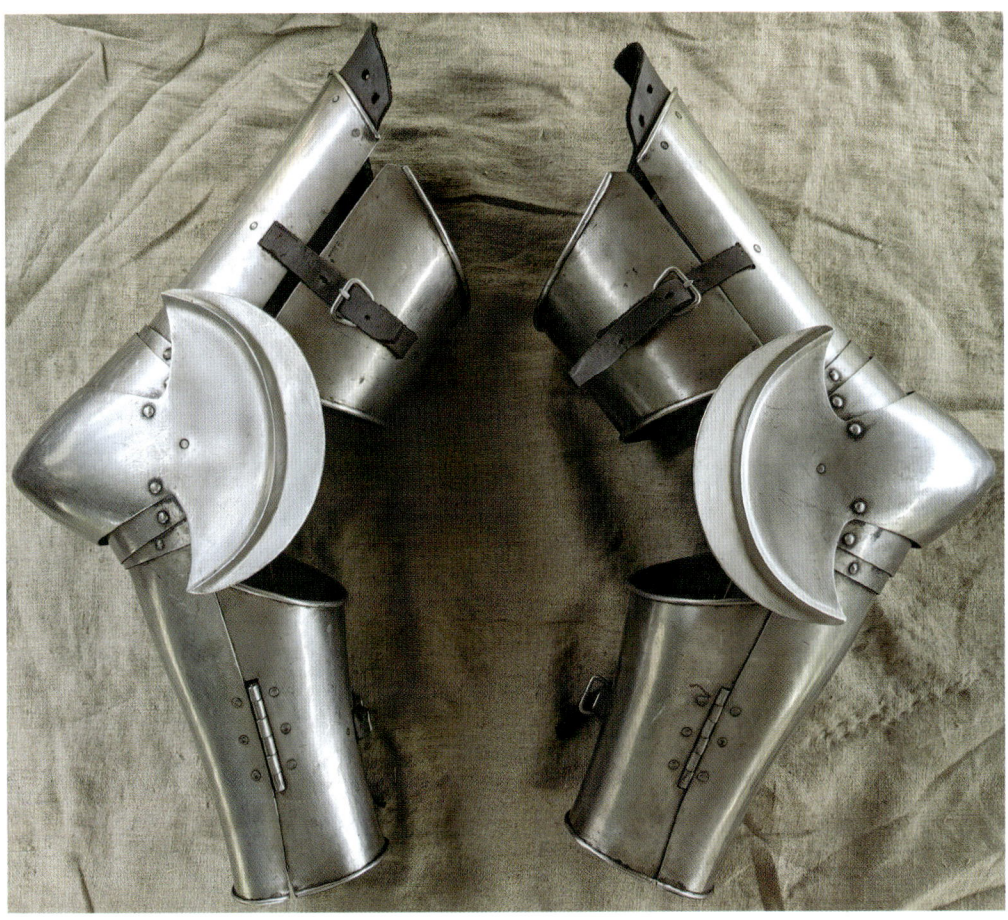

Detail of an armour's *poleyns*. (*Photo and copyright by Genz d'armes 1415*)

century, the personal protection of a knight also included various other elements made from mail, such as *chausses* (armour protecting the legs) and gloves. At that time, separate coifs of mail for protection of the head were not yet in use, the portion of mail armour protecting the head and neck being simply part of the hauberk. The standard conical helmet with nasal of the Normans was still very popular, but a semi-spherical version of it having a full facial mask was becoming increasingly common. During the late twelfth century, due to the increasing use of the crossbow on European fields of battle, most of the knights started to abandon their previous helmets, which had no protection for the face (except for the nasal), and replaced them with new ones having different patterns of facial masks. These were fixed and initially gave protection only to the front part of the face, but they gradually increased in size in order to also cover the sides of the face. As a result of this process, the helmets gradually became full great helms providing complete protection for the head. Regarding shields, there was a progressive transition from the Norman kite

Detail of a knight's leather boot with spur. (*Photo and copyright by Alliance des Lions d'Anjou*)

shield to the new triangular shield that was used for most of the Middle Ages. The main offensive weapons of the knights were the spear and the long sword. Mail was worn over a padded garment known as an *aketon*, which offered additional protection to the wearer. The adoption of closed helmets made it impossible to recognize the identity of a knight on the field of battle; to solve this problem, heraldry saw a rapid growth and each noble family started to develop a distinctive emblem. This was initially painted only on the shield of each knight, but it was later also reproduced on a new piece of garment that came into use: the surcoat. This was worn over the hauberk and initially had no embroidered decorations. Over time, the heraldic display of each knight was completed with the addition of a coloured crest that was placed on top of the helmet. Prior to 1200, war horses were not protected with any specific piece of equipment, but during the early part of the thirteenth century the widespread adoption of the crossbow on the battlefield led to the creation of new defensive elements specifically designed for mounts. Initially, these protected only the head, but were later improved in order to protect the entire body of the horse. They could be made with quilted material or with mail.

The second half of the thirteenth century saw the decisive development of plate armour, which started to be worn in combination with the traditional hauberks. This important process of evolution, like several others, was encouraged by the increasing diffusion and effectiveness of the crossbow. Initially, plate armour was mostly made of *cuir bouilli* (boiled leather) and consisted of disks protecting the shoulders and knees. However, leather soon started to be replaced by metal, and new pieces of plate armour – such as greaves – came into use. The protection of the head and neck, meanwhile, had been improved thanks to the introduction of a hood made of mail – known as a *camail* – that was separated from the hauberk. The torso of the knights started to be protected by a robust coat of plate armour, comprising many small flat pieces of iron that were riveted together inside a thick fabric garment (buckled at the back). During the same period, most of the knights began using maces or axes as an alternative secondary weapon to the long sword. By the beginning of the fourteenth century, the knights' hauberk was usually supplemented by a series of additional defensive elements of plate armour, which could be richly decorated: *vambraces* (armour for the forearm), *cuisses* (thigh armour), gauntlets, *poleyns* (knee armour) and *sabatons* (foot armour). Meanwhile, a new form of open helmet, known as a *chapel de fer*, had become popular. This, being wide-brimmed, was initially designed for the infantry, but as it was much more comfortable to wear than the various models of great helm, the *chapel de fer* was adopted by knights too.

Sergeants were equipped more or less like the knights, but their armour was usually lighter than that of the *milites*. After knights adopted plate armour, for example, most of the sergeants continued to wear simple hauberks. The poorest feudal infantrymen had no military equipment to speak of: they went to war with their ordinary clothes and were mostly armed with their agricultural tools. The luckiest of them had a padded *aketon* and a simple helmet (usually of conical shape, later replaced by the wide-brimmed *chapel de fer*). The foot sergeants and mercenary infantrymen were much better equipped than the peasant levies, all having helmets and frequently wearing a full mail over their *aketon*. Some of them even had *chausses*, while almost all were armed with long pikes that had to be wielded with both hands. The quilted *aketon* – the armour of the poor – was also popular among the archers and crossbowmen. It was usually made of linen or wool, with the stuffing being obtained from various materials such as scrap cloth or horse hair. Quilted hoods for protection of the head were usually worn together with the *aketon*, which during the thirteenth century was improved with the addition of new components like quilted collars or quilted gloves. Some of the feudal infantrymen did not have a shield, but the mercenary foot soldiers were usually equipped with kite-shaped or triangular shields. Archers tended to carry a sword and a knife in addition to their bow; sometimes they could also have a small round shield but they rarely wore armour. Crossbowmen often had hauberks or *aketons*, worn together with a *chapel*

Detail of an infantryman's leather shoes. (*Photo and copyright by La Guerre des Couronnes*)

de fer. Since their main weapon had to be used with both hands, they had no shields and thus were usually deployed behind a line of *pavisiers* – specialized infantry equipped with a large, flat shield known as a *pavise*. The latter became popular in England only during the Hundred Years' War.

By the beginning of the fifteenth century, plate armour had become of universal use in Western Europe, but at the time of the Battle of Azincourt in 1415 it was still worn with large areas of mail, which disappeared only during the following decades. As previously, a padded *aketon* was worn beneath the metal armour, serving to absorb the impact of blows against the plate, as well as to protect its wearer from the discomfort of having metal plates moving directly against his body. By 1430, doublets were serving the same purpose, albeit with gussets of mail sewn on to protect the

Detail of an armour's greave and *sabaton*. (*Photo and copyright by La Guerre des Couronnes*)

areas that the metal plates did not cover (such as the armpits). The most common model of helmet from the late fourteenth century was the *bascinet*, which rose to a prominent point to deflect blows to the head but left the face exposed. Often, a visor could be attached to the front of the helmet for protection of the face; this, in most cases, was of the 'hounskull' type and was detachable (it could be raised or removed for comfort when not in battle). The visors reduced visibility but could have holes in their 'nose', in order to increase the circulation of air, which was very important to reduce the discomfort caused by hot and stale air trapped against the face. Slits in the leather edging of the *camail* passed over pierced lugs (called *vervelles*) on the *bascinet*, which was secured by a wire, thong or cord threaded through the *vervelles*. Another common style of helmet was the kettle helmet, which had the same pointed top as the *bascinet* (although it could be round-topped) and a large sloping brim to deflect blows away from the head and face. The kettle helmet was usually worn together with a *camail* made of mail. 'Frog-mouthed' great helms were also in use, designed to protect

Detail of an armour's *sabaton* with spur. (*Photo and copyright by La Guerre des Couronnes*)

the face at the point of contact in a cavalry charge. By bending forward, their wearers could see ahead, but when sitting upright at the point of impact they effectively closed the helmet's slit and protected the face. Such helmets caused difficulties for the wearer during hand-to-hand fighting, and so were not particularly common. The plate armour protecting the body included a breastplate and a backplate that followed the contours of the body to the waist. They were both constructed from a single piece of plate, although the breastplate could be reinforced with the addition of a plackart across the abdomen. Beneath the waist there was a *fauld*, which included up to seven plates (lames) attached by leather straps. The lames provided flexible protection for the groin area without restricting the movements of the legs. The arms and legs were protected by plate armour that was articulated at the shoulders, elbows and knees. Gauntlets and *sabatons* for the feet were highly articulated, since they had many plates that slid smoothly over each other to permit maximum movement. Plate gussets were worn in addition to mail ones in order to protect the vulnerable armpits. Mail could only be seen on some areas of the body: in the *camail* that protected the throat and in the 'skirt' that protruded below the *fauld* of the plate cuirass. By 1420, plate also started to be used around the throat, either through plates placed over the *camail* or through the use of larger *bascinets* known as *bevoirs*. The latter were fixed to the breastplate and backplate, so the *camail* of mail was no longer used. By the 1440s, the *bascinet* started to be replaced as the most popular model of helmet by the *sallet*, which probably developed in Germany. In essence, the earliest *sallets* were a variant of the *bascinet* that were intended to be worn without visor and *camail*. To protect the

Detail of an armour's *sabatons*. (*Photo and copyright by Genz d'armes 1415*)

face and neck, which were left exposed by the abandonment of the visor and *camail*, the rear of the *bascinet* was curved out into a flange and the sides were drawn forward below the level of the eyes to cover the cheeks. Another change taking place during the later years of the Hundred Years' War was the introduction of breastplates and backplates constructed of several pieces, which increased their wearer's mobility. The *pauldrons* (shoulder armour) were enlarged and started overlapping across the back, while the *faulds* were reduced in number and size, but this was made up for by the introduction of a *tasset* placed over each thigh. Sometimes, especially in England, a second pair of *tassets* was added to the armour (suspended from the hips).

The spear remained as the main weapon of the mounted man-at-arms, with an *arrete* or hook starting to be placed on the right side of each knight's breastplate to prevent the spear from slipping backwards on impact as well as to support some

The triangular shield of a man-at-arms. (*Photo and copyright by Alliance des Lions d'Anjou*)

of the weapon's weight. For dismounted fighting, the most common weapon was the poleaxe, which had a spike and a hammer head; sometimes another spike could be added in order to act as a thrusting point. Axes and maces of various shapes also remained in use. By the 1420s, the standard sword of the men-at-arms had developed into a fine tool designed for thrusting rather than slashing. Its blade was long and tapered to a point, with a flattened diamond-shaped cross-section. Most

The jousting shield of a man-at-arms. (*Photo and copyright by Genz d'armes 1415*)

of the swords were single-handed, but sometimes a second hand could be placed on the grip or even on the blade (indicating that blades were not sharpened all the way to the cross guard). Usually, the sword belt was worn horizontally on the *fauld* of the armour, and in most cases it was highly decorated with enamelled or jewelled panels. A dagger, ideal for hand-to-hand fighting, was suspended on the belt on the opposite side to the sword. The sword belt could sometimes be worn diagonally, from the right waist to the left hip. Scabbards were made of coloured leather and were decorated like the sword belts. Due to the increasing use of plate armour, the large triangular shields employed during the fourteenth century fell out of use during the early years of the fifteenth century. A small buckler shield was occasionally carried, which was designed for dismounted hand-to-hand combat. This was about a foot in diameter and was held in the fist. When held in the hand, it was used to parry blows as an extension of the fist. Plate armour for horses started to develop only during the second half of the fifteenth century, so during the final stages of the Hundred Years' War most of the knights' horses wore just a single metal plate protecting the head. Bards made of mail were quite rare to see, because they limited the mobility of the horses and were expensive to produce. The standard bard made of cloth, which was used in most cases, was decorated with the same heraldic motifs reproduced on the surcoat of the horse's rider.

From the late fourteenth century, most of the infantrymen started to be much better equipped, largely because the traditional feudal levies were replaced with more professional contingents that were often made up of mercenaries. Most of the foot soldiers from the early fifteenth century wore a knee-length padded garment with long sleeves that evolved from the traditional *aketon*. This often had vertical stitching on the body and sleeves, giving the impression of a body-shaped cricket pad. These padded jackets were either constructed of multiple layers of fabric sewn together or could be stuffed with any soft material. Sometimes the richest infantrymen, such as the foot sergeants, could wear a shirt of mail under the padded jacket. A significant number of infantrymen wore *bascinets* without visors or *camails*, but simpler models of helmet were also in use. The most common of these was constructed by attaching small metal plates to an internal frame. This offered a cheap but effective form of protection and could also be constructed using boiled leather plates attached to an internal frame of willow wands. Some of the wealthiest infantrymen equipped themselves with *poleyns* and gauntlets, but these were not common to find among foot troops. Over time, the *bascinets* were replaced by *sallets* and the simpler padded jackets were substituted by *brigandines*, a garment typically made of heavy cloth, canvas or leather and lined internally with small oblong steel plates riveted to the fabric (sometimes with a second layer of fabric on the inside). The *brigandine* could

Small *pavise*-shaped shield.
(*Photo and copyright by Alliance des Lions d'Anjou*)

Infantry shield with complex decorations painted on its surface.
(*Photo and copyright by Genz d'armes 1415*)

be long-sleeved, but in most cases it was sleeveless. It was very flexible and permitted the wearer to have a high degree of mobility. Many *brigandines* had a larger L-shaped plate over the central chest area, which offered additional protection. The rivets attaching the steel plates of each *brigandine* were often decorated or grouped to produce a repeating ornamental pattern. From the early years of the fifteenth century, most of the English infantrymen started to wear a red cross of Saint George on their chests, which was usually sewn into their padded jackets or *brigandines*, whereas the French infantrymen had a white cross. The offensive weapons of the foot soldiers included swords, poleaxes, hammers, axes and mauls. Each infantryman usually also had a dagger, which was employed during close combat. Except for the *pavisiers*, who were equipped with their peculiar body shields, most of the infantry soldiers from the fifteenth century onwards only had a small buckler shield. The English and Welsh archers and the French and Genoese crossbowmen were equipped like all the other infantrymen, except for their main offensive weapons.

The longbow, as we have seen, was the 'national' weapon of England during the Hundred Years' War, despite having been designed in Wales. Thanks to its

Detail of a sword and its scabbard.
(*Photo and copyright by Genz d'ordennance*)

Detail of a knife (left) and dagger (right) with decorated leather scabbards.
(*Photo and copyright by Genz d'ordennance*)

Detail of a falchion and its scabbard. (*Photo and copyright by Genz d'armes 1415*)

Detail of a dagger and its scabbard. (*Photo and copyright by Genz d'armes 1415*)

incredible performance it became the perfect anti-cavalry weapon, enabling the English to emerge victorious in some of the most decisive pitched battles of the period 1337–1453. A standard longbow was 1.8m tall and was usually made of yew. It required a drawing force of as much as 70–80kg and fired arrows about 70cm long with an effective range of between 140 and 300m. Thanks to its impressive power, if used correctly, a longbow could pierce any kind of protective armour from a medium distance. The traditional construction of a longbow began with drying the yew wood for one or two years, after which the bow stave was shaped to have a 'D' cross-section. The outer back of sapwood, approximately flat, followed the natural growth rings and was not thinned (only the bark was removed). The inner belly of the stave consisted of rounded heartwood. The outer sapwood performed better

Detail of a knife and small leather bag. (*Photo and copyright by Genz d'ordennance*)

in tension, while the inner heartwood resisted compression, a combination that formed a natural laminate that was somewhat similar in effect to the construction of composite bows. Bowstrings were made of hemp, flax or silk, and were attached to the wood via horn nocks that fitted onto the ends of the longbow. If protected with a water-resistant coating – usually made of wax, resin or fine tallow – a longbow could continue performing well for a long time. The arrows were made of poplar, ash, beech or hazel wood, and their length could vary from a minimum of 61cm to a maximum of 76cm. The arrowheads, in most cases, had a square cross-section that was up to 11.5cm long and 1cm thick at its widest point. They tapered from the widest point and were specifically designed to pierce armour. Quite often, the arrowheads were barbed in order to make their removal from enemy armour more difficult. The personal equipment of an English longbowman was completed by a bracer made of leather (designed to protect the forearm from the hits of the string), a simple bag or tube made of leather, linen or canvas that acted as a quiver, and a small leather bag that contained reserve arrowheads and the instruments needed to sharpen them.

Detail showing the head of a poleaxe. (*Photo and copyright by Genz d'armes 1415*)

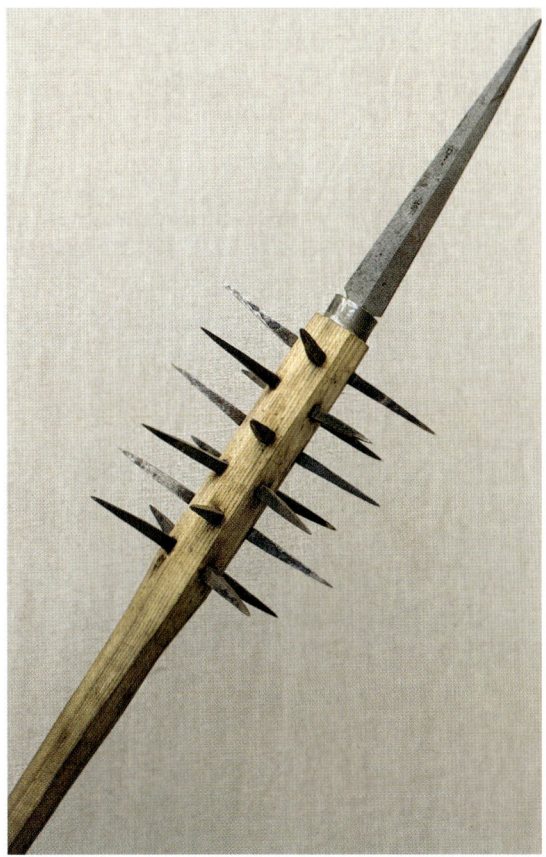

Detail showing the head of a spiked polearm (known as a *plançon*). (*Photo and copyright by Genz d'armes 1415*)

Early handgun from the late fourteenth century. (*Photo and copyright by Genz d'armes 1415*)

Bibliography

Bartlett, R., *England under the Norman and Angevin Kings, 1075–1225* (Oxford University Press, 2003).
Bartlett, C., *English Longbowman, 1330–1515* (Osprey Publishing, 1995).
Bennett, M., *Agincourt 1415* (Osprey Publishing, 1991).
Gravett, C., *English Medieval Knight, 1200–1300* (Osprey Publishing, 2002).
Gravett, C., *English Medieval Knight, 1300–1400* (Osprey Publishing, 2002).
Gravett, C., *English Medieval Knight, 1400–1500* (Osprey Publishing, 2001).
Heath, I., *Armies of Feudal Europe, 1066–1300* (Wargames Research Group, 1989).
Heath, I., *Armies of the Middle Ages, Volume I* (Wargames Research Group, 1982).
Jones, D., *The Plantagenets: The Warrior Kings and Queens who made England* (Viking, 2013).
Knight, P., *Henry V and the Conquest of France, 1416–1453* (Osprey Publishing, 1998).
Loades, M., *The Longbow* (Osprey Publishing, 2013).
Morris, M., *A Great and Terrible King: Edward I and the Forging of Britain* (Pegasus, 2017).
Nicolle, D., *Crécy 1346* (Osprey Publishing, 2000).
Nicolle, D., *French Armies of the Hundred Years' War* (Osprey Publishing, 2000).
Nicolle, D., *Poitiers 1356* (Osprey Publishing, 2004).
Nicolle, D., *The Fall of English France, 1449–1453* (Osprey Publishing, 2012).
Prestwich, M., *Plantagenet England, 1225–1360* (Oxford University Press, 2007).
Rothero, C., *The Armies of Agincourt* (Osprey Publishing, 1981).
Rothero, C., *The Armies of Crécy and Poitiers* (Osprey Publishing, 1981).
Rothero, C., *The Scottish and Welsh Wars, 1250–1400* (Osprey Publishing, 1984).

The Re-enactors who Contributed to this Book

Alliance des Lions d'Anjou

The Alliance des Lions d'Anjou is a medieval re-enactment and cultural mediation company reproducing events from the late Middle Ages. We re-enact two historical periods: the early fifteenth century (1415–1434) and the late fifteenth century (1470–1480), each with its own specific particularities. Our association, founded in 2002, is driven by a shared passion for this period, which is rich in history, knights and fortified castles. The purpose of the association is to share knowledge with the public through the presentation of a war camp from the late Middle Ages. Our military camp showcases the art of warfare in the fifteenth century: life in a war camp, fights between knights and men-at-arms, educational displays of weapons and armour, presentations and demonstrations of gunpowder weapons, children's activities and an introduction to the use of polearm weapons. We also offer educational activities focusing on trade in the late Middle Ages along the silk and spice routes, dishes and tableware in the Middle Ages, hygiene and daily life, and clothing. Our members come together in a spirit of fellowship, sharing their knowledge and supporting each other. We meet regularly for medieval fencing training and organize theme days during which we exchange knowledge and advice. We take part in gatherings of medieval companies in France and around Europe, where we exchange ideas with other enthusiasts and associations. These gatherings take us to emblematic historic sites.

Contacts:
Website: https://www.alliancedeslionsdanjou.fr/
Email: alliance.lionsdanjou@hotmail.fr
Facebook: https://www.facebook.com/alliancelionsdanjou/

Alsatiae Protectores

Alsatiae Protectores is a French group based in Alsace reconstructing the period between 1380–1420. For us, history is a discipline that can be alive. We want to offer our members and our public a real experience of historical immersion. We try to recreate as faithfully as possible the life of contemporaries of this period, civilians, craftsmen and soldiers, who worked within the household of a lord. We present this daily life through crafting, cooking, sleeping, clothing, hygiene, etc., far from received ideas and clichés, relying on a long work of research and archaeological and historical documentation. Our region has an important place in the intrigues and power issues of the Holy Roman Empire and has seen several major events at the end of the fourteenth century, like the battle of Sempach (Switzerland) in 1386, during which a large majority of the Alsatian nobility lost their lives as well as many lords who came to support the Duke of Austria. A disastrous battle that already resonated ahead of other major conflicts, which would follow in other provinces such as Azincourt. Alsace is also a region particularly rich in terms of castle heritage, which is why we also wish to protect and promote it by giving life to these sites through our re-enactment work, as we do by camping several times a year in different castles, including the best known, the Haut-Koenigsbourg castle. However, our activity is not limited to our region because we present ourselves on several big re-enactment events, in France and across Europe.

Contacts:
Website: https://www.alsatiaeprotectores.com/
Email: alsatiaeprotectores@gmail.com
Facebook: https://www.facebook.com/AlsatiaeProtectores/

Genz d'armes 1415

The Genz d'armes 1415 association does its utmost to strictly and accurately recreate the civilian and military daily life in the company of provost marshal Gallois de Fougières under the reign of King Charles VI of France (1380–1422), and more specifically around the time of the Battle of Azincourt (1415). Far from following the cliches and approximations, we try, based on scientifically reliable sources, to come as close as possible to the material reality of the specific time period in order to make our re-enactments as authentic as possible, from our costumes to our kit. Bringing to life martial characters such as squires, crossbowmen and pikemen, but also religious characters along with artisans and their families, we add a role-playing dimension that allows greater immersion for both ourselves and the public. The Genz d'armes 1415 company participates in re-enactments of battles as well as enlivening historical sites, where the members can each share their passion and knowledge with the public.

Contacts:
Email: genzdarmes.1415@gmail.com
Facebook: https://www.facebook.com/genzdarmes1415/

Genz d'ordennance

Genz d'Ordennance is a French association with the objective of re-enacting the Burgundian pikeman (*piquenaire*) as described in the Ordinance of Bohain in Vermandois, promulgated by Charles the Bold in 1472. The group consists of around ten members spread between France and Belgium and gathers several times a year for educational outings or events without an audience. Members of the association are typically seasoned veterans of historical re-enactment who have aimed for a relatively high level of rigor. The re-enactment project itself has deliberately been kept concise to allow for maximum focus of efforts within a specific thematic framework. Regarding equipment, the association opts for sobriety and simplicity to replicate the conditions that medieval soldiers might have encountered. The pikemen's equipment is thus reduced to the bare minimum, and the men are accommodated six to a common shelter.

Contacts:
Email: genzdordennance@hotmail.fr
Facebook: https://www.facebook.com/genzdordennance/

La Guerre des Couronnes

As a living history association, La Guerre des Couronnes offers, through a dynamic museum, a plausible reconstruction of the camp life of a French lord and his vassals at the end of the Middle Ages, from 1380–1410. Ferry 1st of Lorraine, Count of Vaudémont, who was born in 1368 and died in 1415 at the Battle of Azincourt, is the prism through which we approach the various fields of investigation for our re-enactment. Through the research of biographical elements, heraldry, sigillography (the study of seals in documents) and the compilation of iconographic and historical data related to this lord, the places and the time in which he lived, we are able to present the results of this work by setting up a camp, with a lordly tent and those of the vassals all fitted out. A country kitchen where meals are prepared in accordance with the culinary standards of the time is part of this ensemble. A jousting arena is erected for courteous martial contests under the watchful eyes of the ladies. Workshops in wood carving, stained glass, embroidery, aiguillette making and calligraphy bring the camp to life. Presentations such as pay distribution, displays, and sword, lance, axe, and dagger fights are implemented, both in duels and in mass. The members of the company move and show these activities dressed and armed according to the aesthetic canons of the relative historical period.

Contacts:
Email: laguerredescouronnes@gmail.com
Facebook: https://www.facebook.com/laguerredescouronnes/

Les Lions du Kent

Les Lions du Kent (Lions of Kent) is a non-profit re-enactment organization based in Toulouse (south-west of France). We reconstruct the House of an English Lord, Sir Edmund Grey of Ruthin, during his participation as captain of an English incursion in Aquitaine (south-west France). At that time in the French Kingdom, the Dauphin Louis XI was in a struggle of power with his father King Charles VII of France and organized with the Barons a revolt called 'La Praguerie'. Since 1439 the Plantagenets were trying to maintain their influence in Gascony, which was threatened by regular incursions of French forces supported by local noblemen as the House of Albret. Led by Johan Holland, Earl of Huntingdon, an army of 2,300 men arrived in Aquitaine, holding a siege at Tartas and regaining control of the city. Sir Edmund Grey, our protagonist (and the nephew of Jon Holland) took part in this expedition as one of the six captains of the indenture. He nevertheless had to come back to England rapidly: his grandfather had died and he had to take control of his heritage as soon as possible. Most of our members have practiced historical archery, since it was particularly important in Medieval England as a core tactical army corps and a proper social order. It was in fact one of the main bases of military recruitment. We also practice Historical European Martial Arts (HEMA). We are rigorous amateurs and we give much importance to the right gesture as it is described in combat manuscripts or illuminations. It is with the same passion that we are reconstructing, either by ourselves or with the help of the finest craftsmen, the following elements: armour, weapons, clothes and everyday life artefacts based on archaeological sources and academic publications. We are proud to display living history to museums, famous fortresses, history research symposiums and to the general public.

Contacts:
Email: Lionsdukent@gmail.com
Facebook: https://www.facebook.com/lionsdukent/

The Free Company of Aquitaine

The Free Company of Aquitaine was formed in 2011 by a group of archers who shared a common interest in the medieval warbow and wished to keep alive the legacy of the medieval military archer through the research, practice and demonstration of the skills required to shoot the bows made famous by English and Welsh archers during the period later known as the Hundred Years' War (1337–1453). So, why the name? A free company was a late medieval army of mercenaries acting independently of any government, and thus 'free'. The term 'free company' is most often applied to those companies of soldiers which formed in France and Italy during the suspension of formal hostilities between the armies of England and France after the Treaty of Brétigny in 1360. Our group represents a typical band of English archers and men-at-arms that may have sought employment in such a company in Aquitaine during the late fourteenth century. From late spring to early autumn, The Free Company attends medieval festivals in England, Wales and occasionally on the Continent. Alongside displays of archery, our authentic encampment allows the public to meet the archers as they go about their business preparing for war, see the skills of the fletcher and bowyer in action, watch the arming of a knight and get hands-on with an array of swords, polearms and armour.

Contacts:
Email: thefcoa@yahoo.com
Facebook: https://www.facebook.com/FreeCompanyOfAquitaine/

Toxophilus.net

Toxophilus.net, in the person of Christian Birkenbach, presents the English archer in the Hundred Years' War, the Burgundian army and the Wars of the Roses (1337–1485). For over twenty years, I have been dedicated to portraying an authentic English archer, including his equipment and lifestyle, and to my fascination with re-enactment. The focus of my presentation so far has been on the Hundred Years' War. In the future, however, I would like to have a closer look at the Wars of the Roses and develop my account in relation with that era. I am also fascinated by the Burgundian army under Charles the Bold and his dealings with the English archers. This will also be a focus in the future and my portrayal of an English archer in the Burgundian army will be continuously improved. I would also like to take on the challenge of portraying an English archer serving on the *Mary Rose* warship. Unlike many people, I try to combine knowledge about the respective era with practical realization. I attend selected events where I appear as an English archer. I also take part in re-enactment battles and try to test the equipment in practice. Likewise, I am always open to new events and would be delighted to make interesting contacts.

Contacts:
Website: www.toxophilus.net
Facebook: www.facebook.com/toxophilus.net

Index

Alexander II of Scotland, King, 23
Alexander III, Pope, 5
Alfonso II of Aragon, 8
Alfonso VIII of Castile, 18

Baldwin IX of Flanders, 12
Bernard VII of Armagnac, 101

Charles of Alençon, 62
Conan III of Brittany, 4

Eustace the Monk, 27–8

Ferdinand of Flanders, 18

Henry of Bolingbroke, 96
Henry of Lancaster, 70, 74
Hugh X of Lusignan, 30, 32

Joanna of Flanders, 53
John III of Brittany, 53

John of Berry, 83
John Talbot, 125

Louis of Valois, 100–101

Owain Glyndŵr, 100

Philip the Good of Burgundy, 122

Raymond V of Toulouse, 5
Renaud of Boulogne, 18
Robert III of Artois, 45
Roger Mortimer, 39

Sancho VI of Navarre, 12

Thomas Camoys, 105

William Adelin, 1
William of Wrotham, 16

Dear Reader,

We hope you have enjoyed this book, but why not share your views on social media? You can also follow our pages to see more about our other products: facebook.com/penandswordbooks or follow us on Twitter @penswordbooks

You can also view our products at www.pen-and-sword.co.uk (UK and ROW) or www.penandswordbooks.com (North America).

To keep up to date with our latest releases and online catalogues, please sign up to our newsletter at: www.pen-and-sword.co.uk/newsletter

If you would like a printed catalogue with our latest books, then please email: enquiries@pen-and-sword.co.uk or telephone: 01226 734555 (UK and ROW) or email: uspen-and-sword@casematepublishers.com or telephone: (610) 853-9131 (North America).

We respect your privacy and we will only use personal information to send you information about our products.

Thank you!